TRAVELERS' TALES BOOKS

Country and Regional Guides
America, Australia, Brazil, Central America, China, Cuba, France,
Greece, India, Ireland, Italy, Japan, Mexico, Nepal, Spain, Thailand,
Tibet, Turkey; Alaska, American Southwest, Grand Canyon,
Hawai'i, Hong Kong, Paris, Provence, San Francisco, Tuscany

Women's Travel
A Woman's Europe, Her Fork in the Road, A Woman's Path,
A Woman's Passion for Travel, A Woman's World, Women in the Wild,
A Mother's World, Safety and Security for Women
Who Travel, Gutsy Women, Gutsy Mamas

Body & Soul
The Spiritual Gifts of Travel, The Road Within,
Love & Romance, Food, The Fearless Diner, The Adventure
of Food, The Ultimate Journey, Pilgrimage

Special Interest
Not So Funny When It Happened,
The Gift of Rivers, Shitting Pretty, Testosterone Planet,
Danger!, The Fearless Shopper, The Penny Pincher's
Passport to Luxury Travel, The Gift of Birds, Family Travel,
A Dog's World, There's No Toilet Paper on the Road
Less Traveled, The Gift of Travel, 365 Travel,
Adventures in Wine, Sand in My Bra and Other Misadventures,
Hyenas Laughed at Me and Now I Know Why

Footsteps
Kite Strings of the Southern Cross, The Sword of Heaven,
Storm, Take Me With You, Last Trout in Venice, The Way of
the Wanderer, One Year Off, The Fire Never Dies

Classics
The Royal Road to Romance,
Unbeaten Tracks in Japan, The Rivers Ran East,
Coast to Coast, Trader Horn

The Gift of Travel

INSPIRING STORIES FROM AROUND THE WORLD

TRAVELERS' TALES

The Gift
of Travel

INSPIRING STORIES FROM
AROUND THE WORLD

Edited by

LARRY HABEGGER

JAMES O'REILLY   SEAN O'REILLY

TRAVELERS' TALES

SAN FRANCISCO

Credits and copyright notices for the individual articles in this collection are given starting on page 223.

We have made every effort to trace the ownership of all copyrighted material and to secure permission from copyright holders. In the event of any question arising as to the ownership of any material, we will be pleased to make the necessary correction in future printings. Contact Travelers' Tales, Inc., 330 Townsend Street, Suite 208, San Francisco, California 94107. www.travelerstales.com

Art Direction: Michele Wetherbee/Stefan Gutermuth
Interior design: Kathryn Heflin and Susan Bailey
Page layout by Patty Holden, using the fonts Bembo and Boulevard

Distributed by: Publishers Group West, 1700 Fourth Street, Berkeley, California 94710.

Library of Congress Cataloguing-in-Publication Data

The gift of travel : inspiring stories from around the world / edited by Larry Habegger, James O'Reilly, and Sean O'Reilly. —1st ed.
    p. cm. — (Travelers' Tales)
  ISBN 1-932361-12-X (pbk.)
1. Travel—Anecdotes. I. Habegger, Larry. II. O'Reilly, James, 1953-
III. O'Reilly, Sean. IV. Travelers' Tales guides.
  G465.G535 2004
  910.4—dc22

2004018774

First Edition
Printed in the United States
10 9 8 7 6 5 4 3 2 1

Thou hast made me known to friends whom
I knew not. Thou hast given me seats in
homes not my own. Thou hast brought the
distant near and made a brother of the stranger.

Rabindranath Tagore,
Gitanjali

Table of Contents

Part Three
GOING YOUR OWN WAY

Part Four
IN THE SHADOWS

Part Five
THE LAST WORD

The Gift of Travel: An Introduction

Why do we travel?

We travel in part because the human race was born nomadic. Movement has been an essential part of all human existence, but in this age most people have become settled, at least those of us inhabiting the comfortable zones of the modern world. But dreams of other places, of a freer existence, are never far from our minds, and travel is the greatest symbol of such dreams, dreams that we had as children, imagining ourselves out in the wide world having adventures we were sure would be part of our lives when we were old enough to set off on our own.

Travel breaks through the crust of old experience and reawakens us to the joys, mysteries, and miracles of everyday life. We see new or long-forgotten glimpses of ourselves in the eyes of strangers met along the way; we find new connections with our own history as we marvel at the creations of people who lived hundreds or thousands of years before us; we reach a deeper understanding of ourselves and others as we encounter cultures that approach life from perspectives far different from our own.

Travel is a metaphor for our lives as we move from stage to stage. We are constantly accumulating experience, seeking growth and ultimately wisdom, and travel concentrates this growth by presenting us with challenges and opportunities that we simply miss in our day-to-day lives at home. Being free of our usual responsibilities gives us a fresh framework to absorb the lessons offered by a chaotic train station, an impromptu meal with strangers, a chance conversation with a scholar or street merchant.

For some people travel is an escape from the mundane; for others it's an opportunity to try on a new identity; for still others it's a salve for weary body and soul. But for all, travel is a blessing, a gift from the gods, a catalyst for living a richer life. As one writer says, "Travel messes everything up."

Many of us have been given such gifts, in small and large ways, on our journeys, and this collection of stories, some of our favorites from our award-winning books, shows that we all draw from the same deep well. Go with Pamela Michael to India to discover the unexpected gift she received from a Khan man; travel with Terry Strother to a tiny Indonesian hospital and share her lesson about grace; accompany Moritz Thomsen to Brazil and be moved by the ineffable beauty of street music; see preconceptions crumble with Andrew Bill in the Sinai Desert, and learn one of the best lessons of travel. There are many such moments in these pages, and we hope they inspire you as much as they did us.

Enjoy the journey, and "may blessings shower upon you like rain."

PART ONE

ESSENCE

Mein Gott, Miss Siripan

*Learning a tonal language such as Thai is a
challenge under any circumstances, yet
not without unexpected rewards.*

THERE ARE SEVERAL REASONS WHY PEOPLE STRIVE TO BECOME
fluent in the local language when they go to work in a foreign
country. One is sheer intellectual curiosity; another is the fear of
being left out of a conversation just when it is getting interesting.
Driven entirely by the latter motivation, the first thing I did when
I went to work in Thailand was to look for a language tutor.

Miss Siripan came highly recommended by my next-door
neighbor Mallika. Mallika's version of English was unique and inno-
vative. Much later, I would undersand the reason: her self-taught
English was ingeniously—and directly—translated from Thai.

"I tell you true, Mrs. Su-san, Miss Siripan not can teach you
Thai, not have a day you learn, for sure. This woman better from
every Thai teacher."

True, Mallika went on, Miss Siripan wasn't *exactly* Thai. But she
was practically born in Thailand, and if the boat from China had
gone a little faster, she would have been. "This is the fault of Miss
Siripan?"

Certainly not, I agreed.

Miss Siripan had a Thai name and she spoke perfect Thai, and
she had taught herself both German and English. Miss Siripan

was the smartest person Mallika had ever met. "Never mind what people say."

What did people say?

Mallika waved her hand dismissively. "About how she crazy, about how she a mean woman. She just like a determine woman, that's all, she perfect for you learn talking like a real Thai."

I shall never forget the day Miss Siripan first appeared on my front porch. She stood framed by the screen door, a gaunt woman of about 35 with a fierce, square smile and enormous sunglasses that she never removed. She introduced herself in a startlingly high-pitched voice that rose imperiously at the end of each phrase.

"I have taught many Americans," she said. "Most are dummies. Expecially the men, to my experience. But the women are more lazy, to my experience. What are you thinking about that?"

"Well, I…"

"Never mind. Why are you not inviting me inside your house?"

"Oh, I am sorry. Whatever can I be thinking of…"

"How do I know?"

I opened the door. Miss Siripan slipped out of her shoes, as one always does in Thai homes, strode through the living room, into the dining room, and sat down at the head of the table.

"Sit down, Mrs. Su-san," she gestured graciously. "Thank you. If you are lazy or a dummy, I will not teach you. If you tell a lie to me, I will never come back. If you wish to learn Thai language you must read Thai. Not what you call pho-ne-tic. *Pho-ne-tic* is not good. Make you talk so nobody can know what you say. I teach you Thai alphabet. You talk Thai like a Thai people, not like pho-ne-tic."

"Frankly, Miss Siripan, I thought that perhaps—"

"You perhaps nothing. You want to learn Thai from me, I must be proud when somebody hear you."

She dug around in her huge handbag, finally coming up with a Thai primer. On the first page she pointed out the first letter of the alphabet, *gaw,* which looks like "n" and is equivalent to a hard "g." Above *gaw* was a picture of a big black chicken, *gai.* *Gaw* is for *gai,* just as "a" is for "apple."

"Look at *gaw,*" she commanded, tapping one dagger-like fingernail on the chicken's beak. "American pho-ne-tic say this same 'k' so maybe you go around and never know is *not* same 'k.' Is sound *gaw gaw gaw,* not *kaw kaw kaw* like crow. You want forever say *kai* instead of *gai* when you try to buy chicken and market woman think you say *kai*-egg from letter *kaw* but you only know American pho-ne-tic so you never hear any difference, and Thai people think you not know what, Mrs. Su-san?"

Inside me, a tiny voice was saying, "If this woman is still here in fifteen minutes, you will have agreed to anything."

Thai consonants

ก ข ค ฆ ง จ ฉ ช ซ
ฌ ญ ฎ ฏ ฐ ฑ ฒ ณ ด
ต ถ ท ธ น บ ป ผ ฝ
พ ฟ ภ ม ย ร ล ว ศ
ษ ส ห ฬ อ ฮ

Thai vowels

–ะ –า ◌ั ◌ี ◌ึ ◌ื ◌ุ ◌ู
เ–ะ เ– เ–อะ เ–อ
เ–า เ–อะ เ–ียะ เ–ีย
เ–ือ แ–ะ แ– โ–ะ
โ– ใ– ไ–

The mesmerizing tap of Miss Siripan's amazing fingernail on the chicken's beak continued. "Repeat after me this one sentence." She slowly pronounced a series of sounds, I strained to pronounce them. No mynah bird could have done better.

Why did I try so hard? Was it because I hoped to vindicate my countrymen (dummies) and women (lazies)? Or because I could not—for reasons I couldn't begin to understand—bear to disappoint Miss Siripan?

When I finished, there was a long silence, the first since her arrival.

"Mein Gott!" she exclaimed in a stage whisper, then grasped my hands with excruciating force. *"Mein Gott,* Mrs. Su-san, you have ear! I can't believe it, I finally got a student who hears Thai language. All many damn dummies and lazy women and now, now I am luckiest Thai teacher in Bangkok. You know what you said, Mrs. Su-san?"

"Something about a chicken?"

She roared with laughter and wiped her eyes. "Never mind damn chicken. I just fool you about that. You said, '*I will write Thai language.*'"

Fifteen minutes had not passed. She had hooked me in three.

"Today I tell you twenty letters," she continued, now triumphant. "You say after me until you perfect, then you write one hundred times each letter for homework. I come back tomorrow with more books."

"When will you expect me to have written the twenty letters one hundred times?"

"Why you not listen to me? I said I come back tomorrow. Every day, twenty letters. On fourth day, finish all sixty-four alphabet letters and feel pride and happiness. Then for two weeks practice five tones of Thai language, and make one hundred sentences every day. Then for two months read newspaper and make vocabulary. Then you will be a Thai-speaking person." She sat back and smiled. "Not one hundred percent, but I won't have to be ashamed when somebody hear you."

The weeks passed. Hour after hour, day after day, I copied, memorized, repeated sounds. First letters, then words, then the five tones of the Thai language which are as important as the alphabet itself. To change "horse" to "dog," or "wood" to "new," nothing was required but the rise and fall of the voice.

Three months passed. Then one evening as I stared at the dozens of sheets of homework filled with columns of scribbled words, I was overwhelmed. I had completed only 64 of my mandatory 100 new sentences for the week. My mind was empty. I didn't want to learn anything. I quit, and I didn't *care*.

But the next evening, when I heard Miss Siripan walking up the path, suddenly I cared very, very much. The quite justifiable speech I had rehearsed 20 or 30 times had become a mouthful of ashes.

There was only one sensible thing to do, and I did it. I ran upstairs, locked myself in the bathroom, and told my servant Anong to tell Miss Siripan that I was quite, quite ill.

I had *told a lie.*

Cowering in the bathroom, I heard Miss Siripan speak sharply to Anong. The terrified Anong whimpered in reply and scurried away. Then came the steady pad, pad of Miss Siripan's bare feet on the stairs.

"Mrs. Su-san," she shouted. "You not sick. You not finish sentences. True or false?"

"I…please, not today."

"You see! You afraid make more lies."

I hated myself for the sniffling, squeaking noises that were escaping through the bath towel.

"Sounding like a mouse, Mrs. Su-san," Miss Siripan said. She laughed, softly for her, and said, "I know you are not a dummy, not lazy. Maybe I make too hard for you. I come back tomorrow. You make only, maybe fifty sentences. But no more lies."

"Thank you," I whispered through the door, but didn't unblock it. "I promise I will never lie to you again."

"Stop that mouse crying. Stay in the bathroom so you not have to look at me and lose your face."

Her footsteps faded away, the screen door banged shut. I watched the second hand on my watch go around twice, then unlocked the door. Ever afterword, I would understand the subtle give-and-take of "saving face."

In another month I was truly reading, writing, and speaking Thai. Not 100 percent, but Miss Siripan did not have to be "ashamed for somebody to hear me." Her joy in my progress was almost embarrassing. But my ability to hold up under her will, what had become her total domination of my life, was crumbling. And so I grasped at a feeble excuse, in an attempt to pull away.

"Miss Siripan," I began, keeping my eyes fixed on the newspaper I had been reading aloud to the steady tap-tap of her fingernail. ("Mrs. Su-san! *Thai* rhythm. *Thai* rhythm.") "Miss Siripan, there's something I have to tell you. Really, it's good news."

The tapping stopped abruptly.

"I got a promotion at work." This was true. Whatever excuse I used, it would have to be at least grounded in the truth. "Of course, I'm *thrilled,* and I'm sure you know that a big part of it is all you've done for me."

Silence.

I began babbling. "This will mean I have to work a lot more hours—actually, I'll probably rue the day I got promoted—and I— I hope you will undertand but I am just going to *have* to take a break from studying Thai for a while. Of course, it won't be permanent. I mean, I think I just need a few months."

Miss Siripan sat perfectly still for a moment, then rose slowly from the dining room table with an unbearable smile on her face.

"This is not about promotion, is it? Say so, Mrs. Su-san. *Do not tell a lie to me!*"

"I did get a promotion. I have never lied to you since—since that one time. Oh, Miss Siripan. Please, please *try* to understand."

She began stacking her books neatly. Then she reached swiftly across the table and clutched my shoulders. The force of her grasp was painful. And then, with one awful sob, she snatched up her books and her handbag, and fled.

I did not hear from Miss Siripan for an entire year. During that time, I studied with a friend's auntie who was eager to introduce me to Thai literature. Khun Sangworn was a soft-spoken, lovely lady who amused herself by translating French novels into Thai. Every few years she would take a coterie of young Thai ladies on a cultural tour of Switzerland, France, and Italy.

If Miss Siripan had been, as Mallika described her, "not exactly Thai," Khun Sangworn was quintessentially Thai. The contrast between my first teacher and my second was indescribable.

The first time Miss Siripan came back to visit, she was friendly and polite, and made no mention of our lessons together. Although she made clear that she knew I was studying with someone else, we both smiled our way through the conversation, saving each other's face.

Every month or so thereafter, she would drop in unexpectedly for tea. Occasionally she would correct a slip in my Thai, we would laugh, and the sense of strain would fall away. But eventually the visits stopped. I wrote, and my letter was returned "addressee unknown."

I never saw Miss Siripan again.

Over twenty years have passed since I sat across a dining-room table from that remarkable woman, learning to speak Thai with a faintly Chinese-German accent, and reading newspaper articles aloud, frequently interrupted by her high, sharp voice and her shattering laugh.

"Mrs. Su-san, wrong, wrong, wrong! Why you make word for 'revolt' sound like word for 'shrimp paste'? Some revolt. Maybe Mrs. Su-san wants to say about those revolting people. 'Let them eat shrimp paste!'"

"I beg your pardon?"

"What, Mrs. Su-san never study French Revolution?"

"It's not revolting people, Miss Siripan. It's *rebelling.*"

"What is revolting?"

"Actually, shrimp paste is revolting. It smells."

"What you expect? Smell bad because it get old, and smashed with salt."

"Right. So I don't want to eat it. I *rebel…*"

Revolt is ga-*bot*…shrimp paste is ga-*bi*…Never to be forgotten.

I remember particularly one day toward the end of our lessons together, when she appeared with those other books.

"Mrs. Su-san, you speak pretty good Thai now. I have taught you because I had an intelligent idea. If American can read Thai alphabet and make all sounds fluently, that American can use Thai for something important. Here, you copy this."

She scribbled something on a sheet of paper and pushed it toward me.

"But, Miss Siripan, this is a *Chinese character!* What does this have to do with my Thai?"

"Ha, ha! Perfect Thai alphabet with vowel and tone can make pho-ne-tic way for learn Chinese one hundred percent better from English pho-ne-tic for Chinese. English pho-ne-tic smell for learn Thai, smell worse one hundred times for learn Chinese.

Make you speak Chinese like I not know what—"Oi, Mrs. Su-san! You crying? You going to lock yourself in bathroom again?"

She smiled, but then, sensing my mood, she asked, "You angry, Mrs. Su-san?"

"It isn't a matter of angry—I mean anger. I guess I just can't cope with this—this idea of yours."

"Cope?" she frowned. "I do not know this word, *cope.*"

"It means—well, I just can't begin to manage the idea of studying Chinese at this point."

"Ah." Her expression relaxed. "*Manage.* I know about *manage.* Never mind. I manage. You write."

No, Miss Siripan. I wasn't angry. Not then, not now. Wherever you are, I hope you have a student who does not tell lies, and who has an ear, and who, *Mein Gott,* will remember you as fondly as I do.

★

Susan Fulop Kepner teaches Southeast Asian Cultures and Literatures and the Thai language at the University of California, Berkeley. She is the author of The Lioness in Bloom: Modern Thai Fiction about Women, *and the translator of the Thai novel* Letters from Thailand.

PAMELA MICHAEL

The Khan Men of Agra

The author takes a chance in an Indian train station.

ONE GOOD THING ABOUT MONSOONS: THEY SURE KEEP THE DUST down, I thought to myself, peering out the milky window of the Taj Express. I surveyed the approaching station from my uncertain perch between two lurching cars, ready to grab my bag and disembark purposefully. Despite the early hour, the platform slowly scrolling past me was packed with people.

Of the dozen or so bony hands struggling to wrench my suitcase from my grip as I stepped off the train at Agra, perhaps two were porters, four or five were rickshaw drivers, three or four were taxi drivers, and maybe a couple were thieves. The sudden rush of mostly barefoot men in states of undress ranging from rags to britches brought me face to face with the difficulty of "reading" a person's demeanor or intentions in an unfamiliar culture. What to do?

I already knew from my few days in New Delhi that I would have to choose one of these men—not because I didn't want to carry my own bag, but because I would be hounded mercilessly until I paid someone to do it for me. It's a defensive necessity, and an effective hedge for women traveling alone who must rely on their own wits and the unreliable kindness of strangers—the taxi-

11

wallah as protector and guide. In Delhi, though, the competitive tourist market is based more on ingenuity and charm than intimidation. Many of the drivers had developed very engaging come-ons, my favorite being the rickshaw driver who purred, "And which part of the world is suffering in your absence, Madam?"

My reluctance to hire anyone apparently was being interpreted as a bargaining ploy. Several men had begun to yell at each other and gesture toward me, ired by the low rates to which their competitors were sinking for the privilege of snagging a greenhorn tourist fresh off the train. Not wanting to see the end result of such a bidding war, I handed over my bag to the oldest, most decrepit-looking of the bunch, deciding I might be able to outrun (or overtake) him if I had to and also because he had an engaging (if toothless) smile.

Triumphant, he hoisted my bag on top of his turban and beckoned me to follow as he set out across the tracks. For the first few minutes the old man had to fend off a persistent few rival drivers who thought they could convince me to change my mind by casting aspersions on the character, safety record, and vehicle of the man I had chosen, whose name he told me, was Khan, Kallu Khan.

Half way through the station, in a particularly crowded spot, Kallu handed my bag to another (much younger and, I theorized, more fleet-footed) man.

"Hey, wait a minute!" I protested.

"My cousin Iki," Kallu assured me.

"So, what's he doing with my bag?" I asked.

"Helper," I was told.

I went into red-alert and quickened my pace to keep up with Iki and my luggage. As we reached the street it began to rain again, part of the deluge/blue sky monsoon cycle to which I had become accustomed. Over my objections, Iki put my bag in the trunk of their car, a battered Hindustan Ambassador that was unmarked except by mud, no reassuring "Agra Taxi Company" emblazoned on the door.

"Thief might steal suitcase in back seat, Madam," Kallu explained. I acquiesced—the dry shelter of the "taxi" looked inviting and I was worn down by the ceaseless demands on my ability to communicate, decipher, make decisions, find, respond, protect, etc., that travel entails, even in a four-star situation, which the Agra train station was decidedly not.

Once underway, my relief at having escaped the crowd and rain was somewhat dampened by my realization that I was on a rather deserted road with two men who were probably making the same kind of un- and mis-informed assumptions about me that I was making about them. I peered out the rain-streaked window to my right to get my bearings and to take in some of the sites I had come to India to see. I was also tentatively toying with escape options. All I could see was a blur of red, towering overhead and as far into the distance as I could make out. The Red Fort, of course. I had done my homework, so I knew the walls were 70 feet high, surrounded by a moat. On my left was a long stretch of sparse forest, separated from the roadway by a crumbling, low iron fence.

Suddenly, Iki pulled the car over on the left and stopped alongside a broken place in the fence. Kallu got out of the passenger side and opened my door saying, "Now I show you something no tourist ever see, Madam."

"That's all right," I said, "let's just get to the hotel. Tomorrow is better," I demurred.

"Please Madam," he insisted and, sensing my concern about my suitcase, he added, "Don't worry, Iki stay here with your bag."

I was already chastising myself for being so naive and trying to decide how much real danger I was in when I looked—really looked—into Kallu's eyes for the first time. They were kind; kind and bloodshot, but kind. In an instant I made the sort of decision that every traveler has to make from time to time: you decide to take a risk, trust a stranger, enter a cave, explore a trail, act on intuition, and experience something new. It is this giving oneself over to a strange culture

Ambassador sedan

or environment that often reaps the most reward, that makes travel so worthwhile and exhilarating.

As if to affirm my decision, the rain stopped. "OK, Mr. Khan, you show me," I said. We walked down a muddy path through a stand of stilted trees, leaving Iki behind, smoking a *bidi*. My courage faltered a couple of times when I caught a glimpse of a spectral, loin-clothed man through the leaves, but I said nothing and slogged on, hoping for the best.

It came quickly and totally unexpectedly: an enormous mauve river, its banks aflutter with river-washed tattered clothes hanging from poles and vines—work in progress of dhobi-*wallahs*, the laundry men. Directly across the river, luminescent in a moisture-laden haze, was the Taj Mahal, seen from an angle that, to be sure, few tourists ever see and shared with affection by a man who clearly derived great pride from its grandeur. The monument's splendor was all the more striking, its manifest extravagance even more flamboyant in contrast to the faded homespun garments flapping rhythmically in the humid monsoon breeze. We could only stand there and beam at each other on the shores of the mighty Yamuna, the Khan man and I. I like to think it was a sweet kind of victory for us both.

★

Pamela Michael is a freelance writer, radio producer, and education consultant. She is the editor of The Gift of Rivers, *co-editor of* A Mother's World, A Woman's Passion for Travel, *and* Wild Writing Women: Stories of World Travel, *as well as the author of* The Whole World is Watching. *Currently, she is the director of The River of Words Project, which she co-founded with former U.S. Poet Laureate Robert Hass. She lives in Clayton, California.*

THOM ELKJER

No Distance in the Heart

Some knowledge comes from a
place beyond the mind.

THE LITTLE BOY WAS TROTTING AROUND BETWEEN THE BREAK-fast tables in the hotel, his arms wide behind him like airplane wings. His eyes were dark and round, his hair tousled black, his features unmistakably Catalán. I watched him and reflected that I might easily have been home, watching my own child fly about the kitchen. Instead I was in Barcelona, thousands of miles from the small town in California where my wife was probably sleeping.

We had moved away from the city a few weeks earlier, to recover from twin blows: first a miscarriage, then cancer. It appeared now that we would never have children of our own. I also sensed a growing gulf between us, which no amount of loving words or physical tenderness seemed to bridge. It was hard to be away from her but also, I had to admit, a relief.

In Spanish, I asked the boy where he was flying.

"Cataluña," he answered, and looked down at the floor as if from a great height. "Can't you see it?"

An elderly woman at the next table played along, telling the boy that it was too far down for her to see with her old eyes. This brought him up short. He stopped flying and stared at her, as if seeing something terrible in her wrinkled skin and snow white hair. A moment later he ran back to his mother's lap and buried his head in her skirts.

The elderly woman spoke across the tables, apologizing to the boy's mother for scaring him. Her companion, in tweed blazer, patted her hand and consoled her. "You couldn't know," he said to her in a polished British accent. "Lord knows we never had children of our own." Now it was my turn to stare. I dropped some money on the table, picked up my newspaper, and left.

Barcelona seems to me a town full of art directors, with everyone dressed in black with splashes of red. This is especially true in the winter, when chill winds blow down the city's wide streets. The uniform seems to be a black overcoat, with a snow-white scarf and dashing red beret. The Catalans are an elegant people, especially walking together in public, but today I had my eye on the children. Many of them, too, were in black with boldly colored hats or mittens. They capered about, their bright eyes flashing and voices ringing in the cool air. I began to want one of them, any one. I would take the child home to my wife, and we would be parents at last. Surely that would knit us back together.

I finished my appointments, had some coffee in the Café de la Opera, and trudged back up Las Ramblas to Plaza de Cataluña for the train back to my hotel, north of the Diagonal. It was morning in California. My wife would be waking up, maybe reading in bed. I would call her and tell about bringing home a kid from Catalonia. We would laugh together as we embellished the plot. I would feel better.

The platform was not too crowded so I wandered to the edge and looked down. The cars of the Barcelona metro ride three or so feet above the tracks, on springy undercarriages. The platform is even with the floor of the cars, but there is a wide gap between them. Unlike London, however, there is no warning painted on the platform, or loudspeaker constantly intoning "Mind the gap!" Worst of all, the wall of the platform sloped down toward the tracks, so anything that fell over the edge could wind up on the tracks. An accident waiting to happen, I thought, until a little girl in a pink hooded jacket materialized next to me.

This was not a miniature art director, but an open-faced, curious child in soft, little-girl colors. She was three or four years old, steady on her feet except when she was looking up, as she was right now, at me. Her mother struggled with a clutch of parcels and shopping bags. I smiled at her briefly but she was too harried to return it. Instead she spoke sharply to her daughter to stay close. I had been preparing to pat the girl's pig-tailed head, but I slipped my hand back into my pocket.

The girl and her mother got on the same train I did. We boarded mid-car, and the two of them got the last two available seats. I stood up near the door. We passed Grecia and St. Gervasi stations on our way to Reina Elisenda, and all the while I was thinking, this is the child I want. She merrily explored the train without getting in others' way, she kissed her mother impulsively (the only time I saw the woman smile), and chatted amiably with someone, perhaps a cat or dog, that only she could see. Once she looked up at me and smiled. I smiled back. A delightful child.

After the doors of the car closed at Muntaner station, the woman began to gather her parcels and make sure her daughter had her mittens. I realized they were getting off at Bonanova, a station before me, and thought briefly about getting off with them. I didn't really intend to steal the girl, but I wasn't prepared to lose her so soon, either. Then I remembered my wife, back home in bed. I didn't want to miss her before she left for work. I had to get back to the hotel to make my call.

The train stopped and the doors opened. Everyone who was getting off the train left the car. The woman quickly zipped up her daughter's coat and took her hand to walk her off the train. But as they came to the open doorway, just next to me, the little girl pulled her hand free so she could prove to her mother that she could step across the gap herself. Her mother said "no" and snatched at the girl's hand. Instead she got the sleeve of her daughter's coat, just as the girl began to step out of the train.

Looking down, I saw her hands disappear into the sleeves of her coat as her mother pulled it upward. The girl's foot did not reach the platform. The bell rang to announce that the doors were about to close. At the same moment as her mother, who was stepping onto the platform, I realized that the little girl was sliding out of her coat, through the gap, and down onto the tracks beneath the departing train.

Her mother dropped her parcels and yanked harder on the pink hooded jacket, but it was too late for that. I was already on the floor of the car, thrusting my arm down the gap, aiming for the area underneath the girl's coat. I felt skin, grabbed hard, and managed to get hold of the girl's wrist. She was so light that it took just one long pull to bring her out from beneath the train and into the air. The woman snatched her daughter from my one-handed grip an instant before the train doors closed. Now I was on the train, mother and daughter on the platform. The train pulled away.

Looking back, I saw the woman convulsively clutching her daughter to her chest and stroking her hair. Some people on the platform picked up parcels while others pointed toward the train, shouted and gesticulated, or simply clapped their hands. But it was like watching TV with the sound turned off. The doors and windows of the train were sealed shut. I couldn't hear anything but the sound of the train and the pounding of my own heart.

I suddenly remembered the passengers on the train, and turned around to see how many had witnessed the miracle of the girl's salvation. Not a single person was looking at me. They were all reading, or looking out the window, or talking to each other. For a moment I thought they were all pretending, and that they would suddenly begin to buzz about what had happened. They did not. Finally it dawned on me that the partitions by the door of the train, and the shortness of the girl, had concealed everything. No one on the train knew I had saved her life. It was too fast, and too silent. For them it had never happened.

My heart was still beating high in my chest when I got into my room at the hotel. I took off my coat and sat on the bed, seeing again the scene on the platform as the train pulled away from Bonanova station. I had gotten the girl in my hand all right, but only for a second or two. Now she was gone forever. I would not take her home. She would not knit my marriage back together. Hot tears welled up and spilled out of my eyes. I was wiping them away when the phone rang. I mumbled a greeting.

"Oh, thank God," my wife moaned, and then she was crying too. I pulled myself together and asked her what was wrong. She told me she had just woken from a terrifying dream in which I was trapped by my coat beneath the wheels of a train that was about to leave the station. A little girl had pushed me off the platform and I was lying there, unable to get up. She had woken herself up so she would not see me die.

At that point she began to cry all over again. I was too stunned to reply. Instead I forced myself to listen. She was apologizing for pushing me away after the miscarriage and her cancer. She was so afraid I would leave her, she said, that she was unconsciously trying to get it over with. But now she knew she didn't want me to leave. She wanted me to come home. She wanted everything to be all right again.

When I could speak, I told her what had happened to me in the train. Now it was her turn to be speechless. For a long time we were silent, paying hotel international long-distance phone rates to simply be together. We needed to recover from experiencing a similar shock, at virtually the same time, thousands of miles apart. When we began speaking again, it was to promise that I would come home soon, that she would be waiting, and that we would begin again.

In certain native traditions, a life you save belongs to you forever afterward. Five years after that day in Barcelona, I can still see that girl in my mind's eye. She's eight or nine now, her hair is longer, and she looks more like her mother. I see her running toward me on the Paseo de la Bonanova, her arms swept behind her as if they are wings and she is flying high over Cataluña. Indeed she has been mine since the day I met her, the day I learned there is no separation in love, no distance within the heart.

✳

Thom Elkjer is wine editor of Wine Country Living *and editor of* Adventures in Wine: True Stories of Vineyards and Vintages Around the World.

JOEL SIMON

Crossing the
Linguistic Frontera

*A Yucatán bus trip becomes a window
into Mexican life.*

OF ALL THE WAYS TO STUDY SPANISH—BOOKS, TAPES, CLASS-
rooms—the best way to learn is by actually being in a place where
the language permeates communication much as warm air permeates life in the tropics.

Take for example what one would expect to be a simple bus
journey. You arrive at the terminal early in the morning after
downing a piping hot cup of Nescafé. My wife, Kim, and I did
exactly that. We were excited. We were leaving Chetumal, the
ultimate whistle stop without a train. Mostly buses, trucks, and
more buses and trucks stream endlessly through Chetumal going
north into the Yucatán Peninsula, south to Belize, or west towards
Mexico City. Now a free port, this border town has grown around
the intersection of the sea and two main roads, perhaps ancient
Mayan footpaths eventually paved over with commerce, transit,
and time. Near the heart of the intersection, near the heart of the
city itself, was our point of departure, the bus terminal (which
has now been moved three kilometers out of town).

The place was packed. Not only with people, but nearly everything imaginable, and then some, including noise and fumes, in
addition to buses. A nearly infinite line of buses, diagonally parked,

under and beyond the short corrugated metal awning. The buses were all different, obviously different to those who spoke Spanish, yet looking frightfully the same to those of us who didn't. There were no signs. Well, not exactly—the buses themselves had small faded placards which indicated a destination or part thereof. We were bound for the archaeological site of Palenque, perhaps the most beautiful of all Mayan ruins. It wasn't far, just a bus ride away, and well worth the journey, we were told.

We apparently looked as confused as we were, and a sympathetic gentleman approached, and speaking slowly and simply, offered his assistance. In my best attempt at Spanish I asked for the bus to Palenque.

"I'm sorry *señor*, there is no bus to Palenque," came the response.

I looked at Kim for a moment, then remembered my training watching "Jeopardy" as a child, and rephrased my inquiry: "How can we get to Palenque?"

"By bus is a good way," came the answer.

"Well then,…hum…(as I contemplated the apparent and sincere contradiction)…Which bus?" I asked.

The man looked at me kindly, not quite believing the question, but then, comprehension flashing in his bright dark eyes, answered: "Why the bus to Villahermosa of course…there you will find your bus to Palenque."

Ah-ha! Now we were really getting somewhere…. "*Bueno*, then where can we find this bus to Villahermosa?"

Palenque

"Which one?" the man kindly inquired. (I found out later, there were, in fact, several.)

I was determined not to yield to exasperation but my language skills and patience were beginning to wane. "The next one to leave here for Villahermosa," I answered, not even thinking to think over the question.

He flashed a broad smile filled with comprehension, gold-capped teeth and goodwill, pointed confidently down the nearly infinite line of buses, and said, "Down there, just ask for the bus to Villahermosa, the next one should be leaving pretty soon."

Kim looked at me and asked with a nebulous smile, "What did he say?" Summarizing as best I could, I repeated his gesture, and said he said: "This way." With our bags in tow, we slowly wound our way through the loading docks, densely packed with large families, larger bundles, bound and tethered animals, and quiet children, all patiently awaiting the imminent departure of the respective buses. I kept far enough ahead to ask, every now and then, "Villahermosa? Villahermosa?" and then repeating the answer and gesture (always the same) with assurance to Kim. By the time we finally arrived at the bus marked "Villahermosa" I experienced an unexpected sense of achievement, I was learning patience, practice, persistence, and Spanish, *and* we were going to Palenque. I asked the man selling tickets when the bus would be leaving.

"When it is full," he said simply. We happily purchased two tickets, wondering if these were the last two available.

When is a Mexican bus full? It depends on how well you speak Spanish. If you are a novice to this most beautiful of tongues, the bus was already full. Very *full*. Perhaps it was full even before you had your Nescafé. If you have some experience in the language, then you know the bus has only recently been filled. *But*, if you have mastered the nuances of the meaning of full in Spanish or, some would say, the full meaning, then you realize there is still *plenty* of room on the bus.

Full, for a Mexican bus, has nothing to do with the number of seats, or the amount of floor space available for chickens, or the number of babies draped across shoulders, or the square footage available on the roof for loads of bananas and everything else that can be passed up fourteen feet, or the air pressure in the tires—not to mention those clinging to exterior surfaces: side rails, back door, spare tire. True masters of Spanish understand that a Mexican bus is never full. Full is a function of tolerance, and Mexicans are very tolerant people.

So some lingual novices might have thought our bus, a reincarnated American schoolbus, was full, as we headed out across the base of the Yucatán Peninsula from Chetumal towards Palenque. Indeed, it was full, crowned with humanity and recycled cardboard luggage bound with twine and faith. Like the buses of Mexico, cardboard luggage never dies, it just gets reinforced at roadside refueling stops and occasionally in-between. No one minded the squawk of a chicken or two as we settled into the torn and taped vinyl-covered narrow bench seats. Each seat held two and a half derrieres—the half that had no bottom support found stability by leaning against its counterpart from across the aisle. Everyone who spoke Spanish instinctively knew that the famous Mayan corbeled arch had nothing on us.

We rattled and we bounced and we shook and all seemed to be going along quite smoothly until a new noise joined the chorus resounding from the overburdened mechanical beast. At first the sound was barely discernible, a new clink joining numerous other clanks. But the repetitive hammering, feeling perhaps somewhat ignored amidst the other sounds, began to sing more plaintively, until it rang out, a solo voice against a veritable symphony—the brass section, the cast-iron section, the sheet metal section, the fan belt section, the radio static section. Was our vehicle noisy? Ah…no, noise is a function of functioning, a noise is only a noise when it impedes progress.

Even before the concert reached its crescendo, the driver's helper, riding side-saddle on the roof rack aloft and baseball cap to the wind, the one responsible for loading and unloading the multitude of parcels, began one-handed applause against the rear of the vehicle. Slap. Slap. Slap. The driver, seemingly oblivious to everything else, had his ears well-tuned for this sound. We began to decelerate and soon were overtaken by our own dust.

The slap, slap, slapping slowed as we did. Only the churning dust maintained its former speed. Kim returned my inquiring glance, with equal unknowing. Oh good, a chance to learn Spanish! The driver climbed out his window, the roof helper rappelled off the rack, and they conferred, speaking with occasional kicks to the rear tires and tired frame. We held position inside. Few seemed curious about our unscheduled stop. No one was restless. The driver climbed back in, the helper ascended once again to his perch, and off we went…in a wide arc, turned around in a large flat place, and circled to an unmarked Mayan hut set back from the side of the road. And we stopped, engine still running. The bus now pointed back towards Chetumal.

No words were spoken, yet everyone somehow understood. What language was this? Decisions are a function of consensus.

Only the chickens stayed behind. Everyone slowly got off the bus. As though by unspoken command, "Women and children in the hut, men meet at the stern," I joined the men, who formed a casual semicircle at the back of the bus to contemplate our situation. With a loud creak and groan, punctuated by flourishes of undulating rusted metal, the driver lifted the hinged engine cover. There, gently pulsing, grunting, groaning, moaning, hissing, wheezing, and not seizing, packed in dust, dirt, grime, and oil of the ages, was the engine, apparently sounding fine and dandy. A murmur went round the crowd, hands speaking softly amidst punctuating voices and the occasional knowing laugh. The driver slipped the bus in gear, slowly letting out the clutch. Yes, the noise was there. More murmurs escaped from the gang.

A man emerged with a large wrench from the hut, and crawled under the bus. Only his scarred and torn tennis shoes remained visible. Bang, bang, and he called out in terse, rapid phrases. This elicited a few smiles and companion grunts of accord from the group. An even larger wrench came forth from the hut carried by a small boy further dwarfed by its size, and then a heavy rusted bar. More crawling around, bang, bang, bang, more murmurs amongst the team. Finally the man, the wrenches, and the bar, all sporting a fresh coat of ancient oil, dirt, and grime emerged. Our speculation: the size of the problem was a function of the size of the wrench.

Was the bus broken? A Mexican bus is never broken, no matter how broken a newcomer to the language might think it to be. Repair time is just a function of tolerance, both of passengers and of automotive parts. Anger serves no function. In Mexico one is never promised something by a contrived hour—it's never the laundry will be done by noon, it's more like laundry will be done later, when laundry is done. And when you travel, no one is encouraged to rely on arrival by a certain time. The tickets even try to tell you gently—you shall go from point X to point Y—but the time your journey will take is discreetly omitted. One of the great lessons of travel and its most profound joys to the initiated is that traveling takes as long as it takes—no more and no less.

The unmarked Mayan hut, it turned out, was the local mechanic's workshop. It was also his family's home, and impromptu restaurant/café. The interior echoed a sincere and basic lifestyle, cleanly swept dirt floor, wooden benches worn smooth over the years by countless posteriors, and an area reserved for tools (few) and spare parts (many). Miscellaneous used spare parts, everything from engine blocks to alternators, from brake drums to extra cracked windshields, camshafts, transaxles, timing chains, exhaust manifolds, and even a few spare hubcaps were stacked, strewn, and generally piled in corners, both inside and out. Here was a collection of automotive prosthetics designed to fill even the most obscure improvisational need. Unfortunately, we were in a bus, not a car, and the issue of scale could not be ignored. The wife was serving coffee, soft drinks, and rice to anyone wishing. Families had set up camp inside, and were sharing cookies, crackers, *frijoles*, in fact entire multi-course picnics intended for the journey. All were being set up on red checked, blue flowered, or cartooned plastic sheets and given graciously to anyone even remotely expressing an interest. We couldn't avoid the hospitality. We were immersed in it, and as a consequence were learning firsthand both culture and Spanish, its sounds, its flavors, and its generosity.

The mechanic sent his youngest son scampering down the dirt and dust lane. He returned standing astride the back of a pickup truck which he rode like a bronco bustin' cowboy, black hair pulled back by the wind, eyes glistening. By the time he arrived, the drive shaft, the differential, or some such part had been extricated from the bowels of the bus. It was hoisted onto the back of the pick-up truck with great care by its attendants, like a patient onto a gurney. To those who did not speak Spanish it resembled more a corpse on a slab. But *we* knew, those of us learning Spanish knew, that the pickup truck served as a flat-bed paramedic racing off to the operating room rather than a beaten, battered hearse on a one-way trip to the morgue.

In good time the truck returned and all hoped the patient had made a miraculous recovery. The part was soon re-installed with the benefit of much supervisory assistance. The moment of truth had come. The driver climbed back into the bus, inserted the *llave* into the ignition, and turned it. The engine sprang to life. Everyone listened. But above the engine noise, not a sound could be heard. The supervisory team heartily congratulated itself on a job well done. The mechanic then crawled from beneath the bus, brushing off his newest coat of ancient oil and grime. He cracked a quiet smile, and then a beer. Everyone was soon collected from the Mayan hut, all the picnics packed away, all the babies returned to shoulders, all the farewells and thank-yous said and with all the bodies settling back into place, our bus rolled off into the night.

Did we get to Palenque on time? Time is a function of wisdom. The Mexican people are wise enough to know that one should not expect anything by a contrived hour…"on time" translates to "in time," "in due time." We arrived in Palenque and time was still with us, it was there to greet us. In fact, we had the time of our lives.

★

Joel Simon's photo assignments have taken him to all seven continents, including the North Pole, the Antarctic, and 95 countries in between. When not traveling, he's at home in Menlo Park, California, with his wife, Kim, their twin toddlers, their cat, Ichiban, and an itinerant possum named Rover.

DAVID YEADON

Letting Life Happen

A small island village embraces a traveler—and he learns
to love bananas in all their creative renditions.

I LAY BACK IN THE WARM OCEAN AND FLOATED, LOOKING UP AT A
cloudless gold-blue sky.

This was perfection. Two days earlier, fleeing a cold Spanish
winter, I had, impulsively, loaded my VW camper aboard an
enormous ferryboat and plunged southward through Atlantic
storms to the Canary Islands, those remote volcanic blips off the
Sahara coast of Africa.

To be sure, my impetuous escape seemed a little bit crazy. I had
little in the way of cash—just about enough to return the 700 or
so ocean miles to mainland Spain. I knew no one in Gran Canaria,
where I had alighted, and had no place to stay except for my faith-
ful camper. I didn't know how long I planned to stay or where to
go next.

And yet, the island spoke to me. Gently but firmly. "Stay," it
said. "Just stay and see what happens." For a person who loves to
be on the move, it seemed an odd proposition. But the voice
inside sounded so certain, so totally clear. "Stay. Stay and let
things happen."

And so that's what I did. And once I allowed myself to let go,
things literally arranged themselves and I stood around watching

like a delighted spectator as my life on Gran Canaria was fashioned gently before my eyes.

Although the Canary Islands were referred to briefly by Pliny the Elder as the Fortunate Isles, little was known about these remote volcanic outposts until the arrival of explorer Jean de Bethencourt in 1402, who came with plans to establish colonies for the Spanish crown. The Guanches, the islands' only inhabitants, were rousted out of their cave-dwelling languor and eliminated long before Columbus's brief but famous stop-over here on the way to the New World.

Gran Canaria and Tenerife experienced the first great surges of tourist-resort development in the 1960s. Little Lanzarote followed later and now boasts a handful of beach resorts below its moonscape hinterland of volcanoes, lava fields and "black deserts" of sand and ash.

More remote and undiscovered are the tiny islets of Gomera and Hierro, where dense rain forests and terraced mountains mingle with high sheep pastures, towering volcanoes and hidden lava-sand beaches. Nobody could tell me much about them or the other outer islands of La Palma and Fuerteventura. I planned to visit them all once I had gained my shore legs after a few days in Las Palmas, the capital of Gran Canaria.

But things didn't quite work out that way.

As I drove out of Las Palmas, the map of the island open but ignored on the passenger seat, I let my camper take the narrow island roads at whim. It seemed to know where it was going as we climbed high up the slopes of the largest volcano, Valcequello.

I stopped in a pretty mountain village for *tapas* in a tiny blue-painted bar with a vine-shaded patio overlooking the whole island. Here? I wondered. But I kept on moving.

I drove past more villages with lovely little churches and tiny plazas enclosed by neat white-and-lemon stucco buildings, past banana plantations on terraced hillsides, past vast fields of tomatoes and small vineyards. Huge sprays of bougainvillea burst from roadside hedges. The scent of wild herbs rose from the tiny fields sloping down to the ocean.

A tiny cottage appeared with a stone roof in a cleft between two rocks. It had everything: vines, bananas, a small cornfield, two donkeys, blue shutters, and a view over cliffs and black volcanic soil beaches and ceaseless lines of surfing ocean.

Here? I wondered. But still I kept moving.

At dusk, I parked on a patch of grass below the volcanoes. I had some bread, cheese and sausage, and a glass of brandy, and settled down to sleep feeling utterly at peace. Someone else was orchestrating this trip and that was just fine.

Early the next morning as I sat on a rock watching the sun come up, I looked down and saw something I'd not noticed the night before: a tiny white village huddled on top of a rocky promontory that jutted like an ocean liner straight out into the Atlantic. It was different from anything else I'd seen on the island. Most of the villages were straggly affairs, scattered over hillsides like blown confetti. But this place looked light and strong and enduring on 100-foot cliffs. A long flight of steps climbed up to it from a track.

There was no road through the village, just a sinewy path with cubist houses packed together on either side and ending in an area of level rock at the end of the promontory. I could see laundry blowing in the morning breezes; the hillsides below rose steeply from the rocky beach and were smothered in banana trees. It looked completely cut off from the rest of the island. A true haven. Mine!

Somehow the camper groped its way down from the volcano, bouncing and wriggling on cart tracks cut through the brush. I saw no one as we descended.

Close up, the village looked even more dramatic. Scores of white-painted steps rose up the rock to the houses that peered down from their cliff-edge niches. Children were playing in the dust at the base of the steps. They stopped and slowly approached, smiling shyly. A rough hand-painted sign nailed to a tree read "El Roque."

"¡Hola!"

The children grinned. "*Sí, sí, hola. ¡Hola!*"

One of the larger boys came over and shook my hand. And he wouldn't let go. He tugged and pointed to the steps.

"*Mi casa*—my house. You come."

It was an invitation and I accepted.

We all climbed together. The smaller children straggled in a line behind me; I felt like the Pied Piper and even my wheezing at the end of the 130-step climb had a pipe-ish sound to it.

I've never seen a place quite like El Roque before or since. The lime-white cottages clustered tight in medieval fashion on either side of a six-foot-wide stone path that twisted and roller-coasted up and down, following the idiosyncrasies of the promontory's rocky top. I passed a couple of shops the size of broom closets that doubled as rum bars for the men. Crusty bronzed faces peered out curiously from shadowy doorways. Old women, shrouded in black, scurried by.

About halfway down the wriggling street we paused outside of the larger houses facing a ten-foot-high carved wood door decorated with etched brass medallions. The older boy, obviously one of the leaders of my pack of frisky followers, pushed at the door and a panel squeaked open. The rest of the door remained solidly in place.

We entered a dark lobby with bare blue walls and a richly tiled floor. The boy took my hand and gestured to his followers to stay back at the main door. We moved deeper into the house where it was even darker. Then he opened a smaller door and the sunshine rushed in, blinding me.

We were in the living room, simply decorated with small tapestries, a broad oak table on bulbous legs, topped with two fat brass candlesticks encased in wax drippings. Eight dining chairs were placed around the table, their backs and sides carved in high baroque style with vine leaves and grape bunches. Straight ahead were three large windows looking out over a bay of black sand edged by banana plantations and, beyond that, the great cone of Valcequello. The room was filled with light. The windows were open and I could hear birds—canaries, I thought, by their flighty chattering, and mourning doves issuing soft cooing sounds.

The boy's name was Julio. He called out and I could hear someone coming, the swish of sandals on tiles. I was still mesmerized by the view until a figure stepped in front of me and gave a slight curtsy. She was utterly beautiful. "My sister," said Julio in slow English. "She is named María."

The door opened and the room suddenly became much smaller. A great bear of a man entered, hands as big as frying pans and fingers like thick bananas. A bushy mustache covered most of his mouth and curved down, walrus-like, at either side. His hair was as black and bushy as his mustache. A long scar reaching from forehead to jawbone gave him a dangerous look but his eyes were the gentlest blue, shining, exuding welcome without words.

Julio stood up, rake-straight, María gave one of her curtsies and vanished again and I rose to meet the man. "Papá, this is Señor David."

Tomás Feraldes could speak no English but during the next half hour or so I had one of the richest conversations I have ever had with a stranger. His words rumbled from deep in his chest, like boulders tumbling down a ridge. His son acted as interpreter and we talked in baby-language of everything—the village, the banana plantation upon which all the villagers depended for their livelihood, the ocean, the wonderful variety of fish you could catch from the promontory cliffs, the history of Gran Canaria, and the great pride of the islanders in their little green paradise.

"We are of Spain but we are not of Spain," he told me. "We are Canary people. This is our land. This is our country."

The brandy flowed. Little dishes appeared—*calamares* in lemon and garlic, big fat fava beans that we squeezed to pop out the soft flesh, spicy mixes of tomatoes and garlic with chunks of lime-marinated fish, sardines, island cheese, and more brandy.

Then Julio turned to me.

"My father says you will stay here if you wish."

"Here? Where? In this house?"

"No—in another place. My brother's home. He is away in Madrid."

"Where is this house?"

"It is very close. My father says you will come to see your house now. If you wish."

I now knew I had no control over anything. I'd followed my inner voice and let things happen and they were happening so fast and so perfectly I had no wish to impede the flow.

We were outside again in the narrow street. The children were still there, and off we all went, Pied-Piper fashion again, wriggling between the houses. We walked right to the end of the promontory where we all stood on the edge of the cliffs, watching huge waves explode 50 feet in the air and feeling the vibrations through the rock.

Julio nudged me. "This is your house." He was pointing to a small square building, the last house on the rock, white and blue, with a staircase leading up to a red door. On the flat roof I could see plants waving. There were windows everywhere overlooking the beach, the volcano, the broad Atlantic.

Grinning like an idiot again, I followed him up the stairs. He unlocked the door and we walked into one of the most beautiful rooms I have ever seen. Light filled every niche. On the left was a small propane stove, a sink, a big working table and four chairs with straw seats.

The living area was simply furnished—a few scattered rugs, armchairs, low tables, lamps and empty shelves, hungry for books. I could see the bathroom tiled in blue Spanish tiles and then another staircase leading up and out onto the roof with views over everything—the whole village, ocean, mountains, bays....

It was a dream.

"You like your home?" Julio was watching my face.

"Julio, this is the best house I have ever seen."

Moving in was splendid chaos. Every child in the village came to help me carry my belongings from the camper (it looked so tiny from the top of those 130 steps) to the house at the end of the village—clothes, sleeping bag, books, cameras, food, fishing rod, cushions, towels—and my guitar. When the children saw it, they went wild. Compared with the island *timpales,* this was a brute of an instrument, a battered Gibson with a rich deep tone. They were all shouting something at me. Indispensable Julio stepped in again.

"They say play, Señor David. Please."

Oh, what the heck. "Skip, skip, skip to m'Lou…"

I'd used the same song before on one of my journeys and it had worked wonders. The chorus is simple, the melody obvious, and even if you can't get the words straight you can hum and la-la all the way through it. Which is precisely what they did.

Twenty-three little voices sang lustily at the bottom of El Roque's steps, bouncing around in the hot afternoon sun. High above, a crowd of villagers gathered by the wall at the top of the rock began clapping, and then the kids started clapping. Soon the whole bay rang to the sound of this crazy ditty that was utterly meaningless to them and perfect for this impromptu getting-to-know-you celebration on this, my first day in El Roque.

It was four months before I left Gran Canaria. I even managed to tempt my wife, Anne, to put aside her work for a while and join me in my island home.

The villagers were delighted. Once they realized I was married, all attempts had been abandoned to match me up with one of the many eligible females in El Roque (no, Julio's sister, María, was already spoken for). And on the day Anne arrived I invited the whole village to the house for a celebration. I had no idea what a Pandora's box I'd opened with this innocent little gesture.

I'd asked everyone to come over in the evening after their long workday in the banana plantation. Any time after six, I said. Anne and I had prepared some platters of bread and cheese and opened bottles of island wine and rum. Then at 6:30 precisely, there was a knock on the door. It was Julio (he'd long since appointed himself as my social secretary and general factotum).

"Please come. We are all welcoming your Mrs. David."

Anne and I walked out on the platform at the top of our steps and looked down. Faces! Scores of laughing, smiling Canary faces staring up at us, clapping, singing. And everyone was carrying something—we could see cakes, pans of broiled fish, a sack of crabs, banana branches, straw baskets of tomatoes, bottles of wine, more cakes….

"Everyone who comes to the house must bring present," Julio told us. "It is our custom."

I have no idea how we got the whole village of El Roque into our tiny house, but we did. The kitchen, the living room, even the roof was jammed with villagers—many of them we'd never met. Anne and I were buoyed like froth ahead of the surge onto the roof, and we never made it back to the kitchen to serve the simple dishes we'd prepared. Someone carried up the *timpales* and the guitar and off we went into a spree of folk songs that set the whole house bouncing long into the night.

What had been intended as a one-time "Welcome to Anne" occasion became a regular weekly event for the rest of our stay. Every Thursday evening there'd be a "folk-fest" gathering at the house that would leave our voices hoarse and our kitchen table bowed with food. The problem was not in feeding the multitudes but in actually getting rid of all the fish, sausages, tomatoes, bananas, cakes, and wine before the next session on the following Thursday.

The most difficult items were the bananas. They'd bring whole branches with as many as 150 firm green bananas hanging from them. We tried every way we could think of to use them—banana bread, banana cake, banana crepes, banana omelet, banana purée, banana soufflé, fried bananas, banana with garlic (interesting experiment there), and even fish with baked whole bananas. And we still ended up with huge surpluses.

Aside from the rent we insisted on giving Julio's father each month, we were living a cash-free life. We were utterly happy in our village and had no real desire to go anywhere else on the island. I found great satisfaction in painting again, something I'd let slide, and Anne discovered a previously unknown gift for knitting enormous woolen shawls in bright colors.

Every couple of weeks we'd pack a box of these new creations, leap into the camper, and drive the 30 or so bumpy miles back into Las Palmas to sell our work to bored tourists with lots of money and very little to spend it on. Not that we needed the money. But it was rewarding to see people willing to pay real cash for our rooftop creations.

The residents of El Roque were a hard-working bunch. Up by five every morning, the men moved off quietly to tend the banana plantations on the surrounding hillsides while the women cleaned every part of their houses (even the outdoor steps and the pebbles on the main path through the village) before baking, washing, cooking, buying from the peddlers and fish vendors who passed through the village every day. No soap operas or siestas here. Just the solid, daily, dawn-to-dusk ritual that should have left everyone worn out, but in fact seemed to have just the opposite effect.

Our village had dignity, pride, and constant pep. If there were family problems, we never saw them. If there was malicious gossip and back-biting it must have been taking place well off the main path that we walked every day. If there was infidelity and illicit romance, it was done with such craft and guile as to be unnoticeable.

El Roque was a true home, and we became as close to the villagers as our natures could allow. We went fishing and crab hunting with the men (the latter at night with huge torches of reeds dipped in tar that drew the crabs from the rocks like magnets). We worked in the banana plantations, we picked mini-mountains of tomatoes, we painted portraits of the villagers and gave them as gifts, we learned how to prepare the romantic sauces for Canary Island fish dishes, and we even learned to love bananas in all their culinary variations.

In the end, the village brought us a peace and creative energy that we had never experienced before and have only rarely enjoyed since. El Roque is a touchstone for us both—and a place we have vowed to return to one day.

✳

David Yeadon has written and illustrated more than sixteen travel books, including Seasons in Baslica, New York: The Best Places, Backroad Journeys of Southern Europe, The Back of Beyond: Travels to the Wild Places of the Earth, *and* The Way of the Wanderer. *He lives with his wife, Anne, in New York's Hudson Valley.*

ROBERT J. MATTHEWS

* * *

A Simple Touch

Sometimes East and West do meet.

IT WAS ALMOST WINTER, AND NEARING THE END OF MY STAY IN
Nepal, much of my time was occupied with saying good-bye. I had
gotten to know many new people on this particular visit, but those
persons whom I most actively sought out were those whom I had
gotten to know the least.

They were waiters, merchants, black-market money changers;
they were little children and old women who sold single cigarettes
and matches along damp, narrow streets. I certainly did not know
these people as one knows a friend or even an acquaintance, but for
the past several months they had been my landmarks along countless streets and in innumerable restaurants, and they were by now as
familiar to me as any back home. It was this collection of faces,
brief greetings and equally brief conversations that always endeared
Nepal to me.

Upon finding one of these persons prior to my departure, I
rarely would actually say good-bye. Instead, I found that all I really wanted to do was just look at them once more; to memo-
rize them in their world, perhaps foolishly thinking that the
moment could later be recalled with the same life and clarity as
the original.

Sometimes, in my marginal Nepali, I would say that I am returning to my own country. Most often the reply was simply a smile, accompanied by the characteristic little sideways nod of the head which in Nepal means understanding. And that was all.

One person with whom I did speak was an old man I used to see almost every day. He seemed to spend most of his time just sitting in the sun on a small, raised wooden platform next to an outdoor marketplace where aggressive women with clumps of wrinkled and faded rupees in their fists deftly negotiated the cacophonous buying and selling of fruits and vegetables.

The first time I saw him he smiled at me. He said nothing, nor did I stop to speak with him. I recall giving him a rather cursory smile in return, and then continued on my way without another thought. A few days later I saw him again, still seated in the same place. As I passed him he smiled at me again just as he had before. I was taken by how sincere this man's expression was, and also how peaceful he seemed to be. I smiled back and offered the traditional *namaste*, which he returned. I could not quite explain why, but it was that ingenuous smile of his that many times made me detour just to see him and say hello.

Eventually I found that he spoke a few words of English, and sometimes we would have a cigarette together and exchange pleasantries. Sometimes, after dinner, I would walk through the silent streets that were now only sporadically lit by the weak light filtering through greasy restaurant windows. Then I would come upon him, still seated in the same place. He would be sitting quietly, smoking, and sometimes drinking tea out of the ubiquitous glass tumbler that someone had probably bought for him.

One evening, on my way back to my room after dinner, I saw him in his usual spot, and I stopped to say hello. For the first time since I had known him, I glimpsed his feet protruding from under the rough woolen blanket that always covered him. They were severely misshapen and deeply ulcerated, and the toes were unusually short and seemed strangely small for his feet. I remembered having seen similar symptoms during a brief stint of clinical work I had done several years earlier. No doubt it was very difficult for this man to walk, and it was now apparent why so much of his time was spent sitting. He had leprosy.

Some time after this I again stopped to greet him. He smiled and appeared glad to see me. We spoke easily now, he in his broken English, and I in my fractured Nepali. Out of respect I now called him *daju,* or "older brother," as is the custom. The first time I addressed him as *daju* his expression did not change, but from then on he called me *bhai*, or "younger brother," as though he had been doing so for years.

I cannot explain the feeling, but there has always been something exquisitely heartwarming about being referred to as "*bhai*" or "*daju*" by the Nepalis. Perhaps these words were intended to convey nothing more than simple courtesy to a foreigner, but countless times I have been struck by the intimacy these words implied, and the genuine affection with which they were spoken.

We talked for a few more minutes, and when I left I gave him a couple of cigarettes wrapped in a five-rupee note. He accepted this graciously and with dignity. I said good-bye, but resolved to continue to see him until I had to leave.

This I did, and in the course of my last few days in Kathmandu we would talk frequently. I would do as much as I could manage in Nepali, but we usually relied considerably more on English. We sometimes had a glass of tea together in the pale afternoon sun, limiting our conversation to superficial things, but enjoying it nevertheless.

It gets cold at night in November, and prior to leaving I wanted to bring the old man a pair of heavy woolen socks that I had brought for use in the mountains. On my last night in Nepal, I found him sitting in his usual place. It was a very cold night. I approached him and said that tomorrow I was leaving. I then said that I wished to give him my socks. He said nothing. I felt awkward, and as gently as I could I lifted the blanket that covered his legs. I put the socks on what remained of his feet and tried to explain that I would be pleased if he would keep them.

For a long moment he did not speak. I feared that I might have made him uncomfortable, but then he looked at me with marvelous compassion in his eyes and said, "God bless you, *bhai*. No one has touched me in a very long time."

✳

Robert J. Matthews's first trip to Nepal was a logical extension of his lifelong interest in climbing and hiking. However, it was the rich character and spirit of the Nepali people that was responsible for his subsequent visits. He continues to write and teach mathematics in San Francisco where he lives with his cat, and is sustained by an uninterrupted supply of French bread.

JOSEPH DIEDRICH

The Gift

For everything there is a season.

THAT MARCH WAS A BAD TIME TO BE IN PARIS. A HARD, UNPLEAS-
ant wind whipped the branches of the bare trees and drove gusts of
cold rain through the streets. Heavy traffic splashed through pools
of standing water. Huddled pedestrians ducked into doorways. The
taxis had all gone to wherever taxis go when it rains.

I had come to Paris to meet my wife to try to revive a marriage already broken by a year of separation, and it wasn't working. Our favorite little hotel was damp and underheated. Our
favorite little restaurant had lost its Michelin star and deserved to
lose it. My wife and I had changed as well. Too much had been
said and done in the past year. We just couldn't put it together
again. Humpty Dumpty.

To avoid another evening of strained conversation at a table for
two we arranged to have dinner with some old friends who lived
in the 6th *arrondissement*, an Englishman and his delightful American wife. I had heard that she was having some trouble with
leukemia but I hadn't known how bad it was. At dinner we realized two things: that Peggy was dying and that she was someone
whom we both would miss very much. We all tried to keep the
evening light and happy, and we almost succeeded.

My wife and I didn't talk very much on the way back to our hotel. When we got there, we tried to make love in the clammy bed and failed hopelessly. When I finally shut my eyes she was still crying. The next day we went out to Orly and I put her on her plane for London. We promised that we would try again, knowing that we never would, and we never did.

I waited until her plane had left and then I went back into Paris, feeling a black sense of failure, of things not done, of paths not taken. That which I did, I should not have done. That which I should have done, I did not do. I thought of our twelve-year-old in her boarding school in England, of how much she wanted her family back, and of how I had failed her yet again. I didn't know where to go or what to do, and I didn't care. I just gave myself over to my misery and let it lead me where it would.

I remember ordering lunch in a bistro somewhere and leaving it on the table. I remember going to see the Impressionists again and finding the usually vibrant paintings as bleak and as grey as the day outside—and as the man who viewed them. Then I went back to the empty room in the sad little hotel and laid on the bed and tried to weep. I couldn't do that either.

I didn't want to see any of the people I knew in Paris that evening so I ate alone in a *brasserie* near St-Germain. A notice pinned to the wall advertised someone singing Argentine folk songs that evening at a café somewhere, so I wrote down the address and went to hear him. I lived in South America for a while and I know and like Argentine folk music, much of which has a rough, bittersweet feeling that I thought might fit that particular evening.

The café was in a dingy street on the wrong side of the Boulevard St-Michel and stank of brown tobacco. A handful of men in working clothes were drinking silently at the bar. When I asked about the Argentine folk concert the bartender shrugged, pointed to a closed door, and said that it was supposed to be in the back room there. He also supposed that it would start whenever the singer showed up. I ordered a drink and sat down at a table to wait. No one else came into the place.

Then a shabby old man carrying a wet guitar case came in from the street. He went to the bar, drank a cognac in one gulp and said something to the bartender who pointed at me. The old man shook his head sadly and walked over to the closed door.

"We will get started," he said. "Please come in." None of the other men at the bar moved.

"Am I the only one?" I asked the bartender as I paid for my drink.

"The other one is already in there."

A woman in a dark dress was sitting alone in the inner room, which had chairs for perhaps 80 people. Except for a small bulb hanging from a cord over the little stage the place was in gloom. The old man fiddled with his guitar case for a moment, then he said: "My friends, it seems there are only the three of us. Why don't you bring chairs down here and we will sit around this table while I sing. We will make a little party." He paused and cleared his throat. "Perhaps someone could find a bottle of cognac for us?"

I went out for a bottle and a pitcher of water. Then the woman and I moved our chairs down to the little table on the stage where the old man sat. He poured the drinks and raised his glass in salute.

"To Argentina," he said and emptied his glass.

He began with a lovely old song from Cajamarca. His voice was worn and lived in, and fitted the song well. While he sang I had a chance to study the woman next to me. In the dim light she looked to be in her late twenties, slender, and expensively dressed. She sat with a hand held against her cheek, hiding much of her face. What I could see looked lovely. She spoke Spanish like an Argentinean in a soft and cultivated voice.

After a while the old man began to sing some of Jorge Cafrune's songs. Cafrune was a middle-aged, black-bearded, whiskey-voiced drunk who used to sing songs that he wrote himself for drinks and tips in some of the roughest cantinas in the country towns of northern Argentina. Then someone discovered him and brought him on tour to Paris where he became rich and famous overnight. Then he went back to Argentina and fell off a horse while drunk and was killed by a passing car. He left behind some of the most haunting music in South America.

I knew the song the old man was singing, so I joined in. Then the woman, who had scarcely spoken until then, began to sing along in a soft throaty voice. She sang very well.

Her name was Susanna. She told about meeting Cafrune at a party in Buenos Aires and that he was nice until he got drunk, which he did as quickly as possible.

"He was a rough man," she said in her soft voice. "But the songs he wrote—the words, the music—they are pure poetry."

After that Susanna and the old man sang together—she seemed to know all of the old songs—and I joined in when I could. It turned out to be a good party, the three of us, the guitar and the bottle of brandy in the grubby back room.

It was still early when the old man got too drunk to sing any more. The rain had stopped and Susanna and I walked back to the Boul Mich and up the Avenue St-Germain.

"Let's go somewhere else," I said. "This evening is too nice to stop now."

"You have seen my face?" It was more of a statement than a question.

"Yes."

"I am not pretty any more."

"Yes you are."

"It is nice of you to say so, but I know better. The left side, the side towards you, that is how I used to look. The right side, well, I was in a car that crashed and afterwards a fire...." She looked down for a moment, obviously remembering. "It was much worse at first," she went on. "My right cheek was gone and half of

métro stop

my mouth. I couldn't speak intelligibly. I had to be fed with a tube. Since then I have been to the plastic surgeon many times. I have come to Paris to see another one."

"And what does he say?"

"He says that I will need two or three more reconstructive surgeries. After that he can begin with the skin grafts. Maybe four more years. I will never look like I used to look, but at least I won't frighten children any more."

"That's nonsense, Susanna. You are lovely. Everyone past 25 has scars. Yours just happen to be where they can be seen."

She smiled. "All right, have it your way. We don't know each other well enough to bicker. Now let's go in the Rotonde and have café royal. I will buy because I sing better than you do."

Sitting at the table, Susanna looked at me carefully. "Your scars are inside, are they not?"

"Yes."

"And fairly new?"

"Yes."

"*Pues entonces.* Now we will talk no more about scars."

"I'll drink to that," I said. And we did.

We left the Rotonde and went out into the cool night and the quiet street. Susanna's hotel was nearby and I offered to walk with her to the door. We turned off the St-Germain at the Café de Flore and went down the empty street. I don't know why I chose that particular street. There were several ways we could have walked to her hotel.

"Excuse me," Susanna said. She had stopped and was staring at a building across the street. "Number seventeen. That house. That is where my husband had a room when he was a student, and had run away from the killings in Argentina. How did we happen to come here?"

I had wondered if she was married and had begun to hope, very much, that she was not. "Where is he—your husband?" I ventured.

"He was in the car. He died in the crash." She took a deep breath. "Our daughter too. Only she died in the hospital three days later. I was driving and it was my fault and yet I did not die. At least not entirely." She put her hands to her face and began to weep silently. I put my arms around her, rather awkwardly.

"I'm sorry," she said, not moving. "I had almost forgotten about it for a while this evening, which makes it worse somehow. Will you please stay out with me until I can stop behaving like this? I can't face an empty hotel room just yet." She began to shiver. "I'm so cold. Can we go inside somewhere?"

Most of the cafés and the bars were closed for the night, but on the corner ahead the lights were on in a Russian restaurant and the door stood open. We went in. The place was empty except for about a dozen people seated around a long table at the back of the room. A man came out from behind the bar carrying a concertina.

"I am sorry," he said, coming over to us, "but we are closed. This is a private party." Then he looked at Susanna's tear-streaked, ravaged face and said, "But I do not think that we are so closed, pretty lady, that you and your friend cannot sit at this little table here while I bring you some hot borscht and some cold vodka."

We sat at the table in the dimly lit restaurant and ate the borscht and drank the vodka, and after a while Susanna's tears stopped. The people at the long table were singing Russian songs accompanied by the owner on his concertina. The party must have been going on for quite a while, for they were all quite drunk.

We were just getting ready to leave when the door from the street opened and a young man came in alone. He was dressed in black trousers and an open-necked white shirt with a black overcoat slung over his shoulders. He had dark hair, dark eyes, high cheekbones, and was deathly pale. He was also very, very drunk.

Susanna stared at him as he walked by our table. "My god," she whispered. "He's beautiful." And he was.

The people at the party in the back called out to him and he walked carefully over to the long table, drank a proffered glass of vodka neat, draped his overcoat over the back of a chair, and sat. A hush fell over the party. Then he began to sing.

I don't know what it was that he sang. I had never heard such music before and I have never heard it since. Whatever it was—

gypsy, Tatar, Cossack—it was the most beautiful music Susanna and I had ever heard. A cynic would say that it just fit the mood of the night, but I don't think so. The young man had a superb voice. He sat with his eyes closed and his head back and sang songs which told of longing and heartache and loss and loneliness and love and redemption. You didn't need to understand the words. He sang for nearly half an hour. Then he slumped back in his chair, motionless, his eyes still closed.

No one at the party spoke after that. The people stood up, quietly put on their coats, and began to leave. Susanna and I left too.

"I think those songs were meant for me, somehow," she said as we walked through the quiet streets. "I was being egotistical with my sorrow, thinking no one else had ever suffered so. And they have, haven't they?"

"Yes."

"And yet you can go on and find redemption and peace and beauty—and even love if you are lucky."

"Maybe we are lucky," I said, knowing that we were.

Then we turned together, there, in the middle of the empty street, and kissed. We kissed for a long time, feeling the loss and the loneliness and the hopelessness beginning to go.

Then we walked back to Susanna's hotel together.

★

Joseph Diedrich is a retired Pan Am pilot who spends his time traveling, sailing, trekking, and "messing about." This story was the winner of a Paris writing contest sponsored by Travelers' Tales. He and his wife live in Mallorca, Spain.

⋆ ⋆ ⋆

Terry and the Monkey

Forced to take a closer look at local life, the author
takes a step toward enlightenment.

IT SEEMS I WAS NOT MEANT TO LEAVE INDONESIA JUST YET. THE
past three days have been very hectic here. It all started with a
leisurely swim in a small fishing town on the south coast of Java.
We were walking back through a beautiful nature reserve when a
group of monkeys came scampering through. One calmly walked
up, grabbed my leg with both hands, and turning its head to the
side like a little vampire or a rat, sunk its fangs into my leg. With an
absolutely evil look in its quite human-looking eyes, it held my
sarong, glaring up at me and chattering. I slowly backed away and
told my companion, Tad, I'd been bitten. It all happened so quickly
I don't think he knew, or I really, because the desire to deny it was
so strong. We had been told by a doctor in New Zealand to be
particularly careful with animals in Indonesia because of rabies.
He admonished us for not having been vaccinated and warned us
ominously how painful the remedy is. All of this was going
through my mind, bits and pieces of what he'd said. In slow motion, the little vampire scene began playing out over and over as we
stared at my leg with tremendous concentration, hoping to stare
the wound back together.

The following hours crept by like days. Tad went in search of information, a phone, anything useful. I sat in the doctor's waiting room at the local "hospital." In the outer room maybe twenty people sat, squatted, lay in a five-by-seven-foot space with their hand-printed queue number, waiting to see a man at a desk in another small room. They spoke in hushed tones and eventually left, all seeming to clutch the same small bottle of pills regardless of their affliction. Because I was bleeding, I was first ushered into yet a third room, the "operating room," but only after all present removed our shoes at the door, which seemed a rather nice touch though certainly pointless considering that this room was every bit as filthy as the other two. I sat on the operating table on the blood-encrusted sheet as the attendant shuffled through various jars of crude and antique-looking instruments, trying to decide on an appropriate course of action. After I politely (I hoped) rejected a few options that seemed rather hasty, if not downright dangerous, he shrugged, washed out the cut and shuffled me back to the waiting room. I was, of course, terrified. And I felt ridiculous. Others around me were sporting much more serious afflictions, yet everyone smiled, spoke kindly and calmly to one another, shaking hands with everyone (including me) who entered. Everyone smiled. No matter what. So…I smiled. And tried to respond in kind to the young woman who wanted to practice her sketchy English and who, of course, wanted to know my address, occupation, marital status, why I did not have children, how I liked Indonesia.

I knew most of the expected answers by now but it was difficult to concentrate. I couldn't take my eyes off one of my fellow waiters: a small child, perhaps two years old, held in the cloth sling that all parents here use to tote around their children. He was lying in his father's lap, looking up at his smiling face with big, sad, somewhat-glazed eyes. Lying ever so still. Most of his body was an oozing, glistening mass of rawness with bits of charred flesh, like meat left on the barbecue a bit too close to the coals. Surely he was dying. Surely everyone including his parents knew this. Yet all continued to smile and chat and ask how did I like *gado-gado?*

Occasionally someone would get up and go speak with the parents, smiling of course, and rather absent-mindedly stroke the child's unburned face gently. And as the hours crept by, I can't begin to explain why, but it all began to make perfect sense to me. The smiling, the gentleness, the hand shaking, the socializing. I felt very much a part of some mutual understanding of the need for gentleness in the room, in the world, but mostly in the face of helplessness and fear. Like a big "of course" it just settled into my body.

By the time I did get to see the doctor, I didn't even find it odd to go through all the same questions as in the waiting room before: eventually, almost beside the point, why did I happen to be here. His English and my Bahasa Indonesian were both too lacking to go very far, but I did manage to understand that he did not have the rabies serum (no refrigeration) and I would have to go to the nearest large city in hopes of finding some.

At this point, Tad burst through the door. His movements, his loud hurried voice, his urgency was such a contrast to the past few hours. I was startled and stared at him blankly. As he pulled me toward the door, I hurriedly said my goodbyes and politenesses. Tad looked at me as if I were in shock or crazy. In a waiting jeep was a German doctor whom Tad had literally dragged away from his dinner and who had come to rescue me from what every Westerner fears in Indonesia: unsterilized needles. He gave me all the disposable needles in his possession and gravely told me to leave for Bandung (six hours away) as soon as possible.

Tad left in search again, this time for transport, and I waited, this time alone. It was harder waiting alone. I had thought it would be easier. I was frightened and feverish and my wound throbbed ominously. I stared at it, imagining scenes from *Old Yeller*, imagining invading rabies creeping slowly up my leg. I was tired and it was late. But each time I shut my eyes I was engulfed by a sea of monkeys grabbing at me with tiny hands. Pulling, clutching, ripping, and gobbling, fangs flashing, eyes glowing, and everywhere—the hands. I would silently scream and open my eyes and purposefully give myself a pep talk full of grown-up logic. But it was useless. A new archetype had entered solidly into my repertoire of haunts and private demons. The stuff nightmares are made of.

Tad returned after midnight with tickets secured for the ride to Bandung at 6 a.m. Poor Tad, I don't think he slept at all for nearly 36 hours between his anxiety and my nightmares. I remember feeling glad it was me instead of him because it seemed easier to be in the center of this fear than on the outside, a spectator of sorts.

We found the Bandung rabies clinic. Although I felt immediately comfortable with the doctor and with the quality of care, it took a bit of convincing for Tad. Time was also a factor. I managed to get most of my questions answered and more important to me, I felt in good hands with Stephen S. (as his name tag read), the doctor. He was a gentle, soft-spoken man with no trace of ego invested in his occupation. His calm, happy manner colored his environment and rubbed off on those around him. There was one unsettling moment when his assistant walked toward me with the largest, most unsavory needle I'd ever seen (Tad later told me my face went white), but it was for the dog behind me who didn't seem to mind. The medical profession here is necessarily unspecialized and animals and people alike waited together to see the doctor.

Monsoon season in Java is solidly underway. Even when it's not raining I breathe wetness. The worst part was not the shots, but the new nightmare images that took up residence in my psyche, touching a deep chord in me. As though some unacknowledged fear living inside me finally had found the perfect symbol, the vehicle for expression, in the tiny hands of the monkey. Serving as an antidote to this fear is the overall experience of this country and the calmness it leaves in me. The Balinese tending the rice fields...the man who wrapped packages outside the post office in Yogyakarta, sewing cloth around the boxes with such care...the way the Javanese laugh when confronted with calamity.... Their desire to help is so much more natural and easy, even with the language difference, than my ability to express thanks. It is the gentleness, spirituality, and beauty of the people that will stay with me forever.

*

Terry Strother is a university administrator who lives in New York City with her husband and daughter. This story won first place in the Travelers' Tales writing contest.

In a Soldier's Care

A guardian angel with a phrasebook
keeps watch over a traveler.

THE WISH TO HAVE MY LIFE ORCHESTRATED AS IF IT WERE A FILM was fulfilled in Verona, Italy, the summer I turned 21.

I was part of a summer program for young musicians that was held in this city of golden light and arched bridges. We were housed in a magnificent old building with high ceilings and windows so large I could curl up on a windowsill for a nap.

The building's old stones kept the secrets of countless people who had lived in the rooms, but they could not keep out the awareness that for centuries, human dramas had been played out within the walls.

Dedicated to their art, the young musicians in the summer program were up before dawn perfecting their pieces and I awoke to the gentle melodies of Vivaldi, Bach, and Stravinsky. While I dressed, Lalo played in the background and while eating breakfast, gypsy music urged me to hurry up, there was much life to be lived.

But it was the melancholy music that best expressed my state of mind. Not a musician myself, I had been invited to the program to study photography and my teacher had never shown up. All the other students were musicians who studied and practiced all day and so most of my time was spent alone. I couldn't speak a word of Italian and wandered the streets with my camera longing for someone to share the discovery of hidden restaurants, unexpected frescos, the brooding statues in the cemeteries and the celestial art in the churches.

After a couple of weeks of wandering down winding streets and weaving in and out of alleys, I had the odd sensation that I was being followed. I'd walk faster, turn a corner and abruptly stop, looking back, hoping to catch someone. There was never anyone in sight. Yet the feeling persisted.

After a few days of this, I took a seat outside a small cafe on a dead end street and decided to sip lemon sodas until I was certain there was no one pursuing me. I passed two hours looking at pictures in an Italian newspaper, writing letters, and photographing children who played nearby. When I had just about given up the notion that I was being followed, a dark, handsome man in a military uniform quietly slipped into the seat beside me. He gestured to my camera. Assuming he wanted his picture taken, I picked it up. He put his hand over mine briefly, shook his head, and pulled an Italian-English dictionary out of his back pocket.

For over an hour, we took turns looking up words and pointing them out to each other, trying to communicate.

He was intrigued that I was an American and wanted to know why I was in Verona. He was a soldier serving his mandatory tour of duty. He took off his hat and showed me a series of lines he'd written under the brim to keep track of how many months he had been in the service. Altogether, he would have to serve fifteen months.

I asked if he had been following me. He leaned forward, took my hand, looked into my eyes. I melted. Would he kiss me? We were total strangers, couldn't even understand each other's language, but we had found each other. Ah, for a student nearby to fill the air with triumphant music.

But there was no kiss. He dropped my hand and went back to the dictionary. "Alone. Dangerous. Bad. Places. Hurt. Protect. Duty." How sweet. He was concerned about me and had decided to be my bodyguard.

I took the dictionary in turn. Pointed out "Thank you. No fear. Safe."

He shook his head, tipped his hat. "No safe," he said.

I pointed to my watch. He nodded. We both rose, and he walked me back to the building in which I was staying.

"Care," he said, and gestured to himself, then to me.

True to his word, he began looking out for me. When I left in the morning, he was outside waiting for me. Sometimes he would walk beside me, sometimes a block or so behind. Sometimes we would have a lemon soda together and he would insist I order them so he could laugh with the waiter over the odd way I pronounced the word "lemon." Sometimes I would think I was alone, but would turn around and find him there. Sometimes he was with another soldier or two, but usually he was alone.

We found out little things about each other. He had a large family, just like me. He wanted to go to college, to do something great with his life, but first he had to get out of the military. He would like to go to the U.S. where mail is delivered at the same time every day. We both loved ice cream and he thought eating pizza with hands was a good idea no matter what everyone else in his country thought.

He told me what was good and not so good to order in restaurants, and took me to places he thought I would want to photograph.

I was no longer lonely and the melancholy music that used to define my life in Italy no longer fit. I begged the music students to play gypsy music and pieces fast and joyful.

The other students noticed that the soldier was often near me, and one of the students followed us to a park and took out his violin and played while my soldier and I ate fruit and freshly baked bread.

Time passed too quickly and there were but a few days left. I wondered if I was nothing more than someone to watch over or if my soldier was falling for me as I was for him. But I was too shy to ask and certainly would never make the first move.

He knew when I would leave, and on my last day asked what we should do that night. I took his dictionary and pointed out words. "Group. Students. Opera. Late."

His face lit up. Perhaps he did not understand. I pointed out more words. "Must go. Not alone. Home. Leave. Early." The word for tomorrow I knew. *"Domani."*

He grinned, took my hand, held it for a minute and raised it to his lips. "Good-bye," he said in English. "For now."

That was it, then? He was content to say good-bye, leaving with the suggestions that we might meet again some day? I was devastated.

That night all the students and teachers went to the opera. Ah, how lovely it was, held in an amphitheater over 2,000 years old. The costumes were magnificent. The music almost too beautiful to bear. But I could not lose myself in it when I knew I would not see my soldier again. I tried not to cry, but a tear or two slipped down my cheek.

I felt a hand on my shoulder and looked up. My soldier!

He handed me a rose and motioned for me to follow him. I didn't hesitate. He led me to a higher seat where the breeze moved the music through the air. The opera came to life as we sat hand-in-hand, shoulder-to-shoulder. When the final curtain came down and the crowd rose to their feet, he leaned forward and kissed me to the sound of a full-house clapping. The applause, no doubt intended for the opera, was, in my heart, intended solely for my soldier and me.

He slipped a piece of paper into my hand, kissed me again, and walked me back home. He kissed me once more at the door. A long kiss, one that would linger for the rest of my life.

Later that night, when everyone slept, I climbed up on the windowsill and read the note he had given me by moonlight. "Always. Remember. *Domani.* Love."

I have never forgotten, and whenever I hear the sweet notes of a violin, I can feel my soldier following.

✽

Nancy Hill is a writer and photographer living in Portland, Oregon, dreaming of adventure while living days of practicality. But change is always just around the corner.

PART TWO

Some Things To Do

Seeing Red

In a Spanish tomato war, catharsis.

I AM A BOSOM FRIEND OF THE MATURING SUN, BEING NEARLY 40 and autumn my favorite time of year. In England in the early morning there are heavy dews on the grass that soak insidiously through the leather of one's shoes, the temperature settles to a soft warmth that has just the slightest suspicion of a chill, and the apples fall to the ground, revealing themselves to have been partially explored already by finches and wasps.

Autumn has its pitfalls as well as its windfalls, of course. Perhaps the largest problem is knowing what to do with the glut of vegetables and fruit from the summer's harvest. One thing you can do is pile the surplus into huge heaps and have a festival. In August on the Isle of Wight, just off the south coast of England, they hold a garlic orgy. There was a time, fewer than twenty years ago, when only nostalgic immigrants and anarchist intellectuals ate garlic in England, but European travel has so transformed our palate that there now exist intransigent fanatics who are convinced that garlic is a greater part of the meaning of life. I confess that I am one of these people; I have been known to put garlic on my poached eggs in the morning, and I fully understand why the people of the island see fit to crown a queen for the day and wheel her about in a carriage shaped like a giant bulb of garlic. This is entirely sane and reasonable. In Braga, Portugal, they have a ceremony in which they pass leeks around for one another to sniff; and in Porto, another town in Portugal, they have a rather less dignified celebration in which they thwack one another with the same vegetable. Before writing off the Portuguese as idiosyncratic, however, readers are advised to peel off the outer layer of a leek and try both rituals for themselves. The leek really has a pleasant smell, and it is ideal for the cathartic striking of people without hurting them very much.

But Spain tops all of Europe with its multitude of appealing fiestas. It is important to note that the Spanish are not in the business of fabricating folklore for the benefit of the tourist industry. Visitors are supposed to make do with silly songs like "O La Paloma Blanca" and "Viva España" in the armpits and orifices of otherwise pleasant places like Málaga and Fuengirola, whilst the traditional rites go on elsewhere as they have always done, solely for the entertainment of the natives. In Seville the girls would come out in the evenings to dance *sevillanas,* and the people of Ulldecona would still perform weekly passion plays during Lent, whether or not there were any cameras to snap them.

I have had firsthand experience of this cheerful disregard for the potential of tourism. I was off to Buñol to witness La Tomatina, a particularly picturesque fiesta fortuitously developed to celebrate autumn and its overabundance of tomatoes. I telephoned the Spanish Tourist Office in London in order to ask about it. "Oh," said the man, "there so many fiestas in Espain, all Espain is one big fiesta."

"So you don't know anything about the fiesta in Buñol?"

"I think is in Balencia. I gib you number of Municipal Tourist office in Balencia."

There was an animated conversation in the Valencia office as they discussed the correct answers to my garbled questions. Yes, it was on the 31st of August. Yes, Valencia was the nearest airport. No, there were no hotels, campsites, or *pensiones* in Buñol. "But don't worry, Señor, because nobody will be sleeping anyway, okay?"

✳

It was 104 degrees when I arrived in Valencia, and the people were feeling unjustly persecuted. I was repeatedly informed that it was supposed to be cool in the evening and that it was never this hot. "This is not natural," they exclaimed as they mopped their faces. Of course in August most of the Spanish go on holiday to somewhere nice and cool, such as Galicia, and leave the hotter areas to bewildered and sweltering tourists from northern Europe, who wonder why there's no one about and why there are actually dogs asleep in the public drinking fountains, up to their necks in water.

I was a little hotter than most, given that the extractor fan for my hostel's air-conditioning system was right outside my room and was blasting hot air straight into my window. Take my advice: don't book Room 104 of the Hospederia Pilar; you will boil in your own blood like some peppery Eastern European sausage. Even in the relative cool of the streets (105 degrees) the humidity was so extreme that one expected to see shoals of lugubrious cuttlefish swimming past one's eyes on their way to the sea. I quaffed one and a half liters of water with each meal and bought more in the market, resigned to the curious way in which I am accompanied by freakish heat waves whenever I travel. In Crete once, in the early spring, it was so hot that I was forced to run like a commando from the shade of one stone to another as I attempted to admire the palace of Knossos, and the skin on the top of my head peeled off within a single day. In Cephalonia, I suffered a wondrous heat-stroke that left me so delirious I could not determine whether I was freezing cold or frizzled to a cinder. I declare that Valencia was peanuts by comparison, and whilst the city snored at siesta time I patrolled the somnolent streets on my own like the mad dog and Englishman that I am.

At night it was simply too humid to sleep, so I read tirelessly, relishing the aftertaste of the wonderful cuisine. Four travel tips: 1) You can't get a *paella* unless there are at least two of you. I spent a lot of time looking for spare people who wanted *paella*. 2) There is a dish called *conejo al ajillo*, which consists of whole cloves of garlic roasted with potatoes and rabbit. It makes your urine smell of garlic for three days and leaves you feeling so ecstatic that you don't care that you can't sleep and are being gnawed to death by relentless and invisible mosquitoes. If you don't like garlic, or disapprove of extreme happiness on religious or moral grounds, try the grilled sole. It will make you only very happy. 3) If you want the very best service, including free liqueurs and bonbons, just place a notebook at the side of your plate and make the occasional note in it. The proprietor will suspect that you are a restaurant critic and will act accordingly. 4) People taking photographs of their meals are not critics; they are from the United States.

When I was not eating, I made sincere efforts to find out about the tomato festival in Buñol. In the municipal tourist office there was a young woman with beautiful eyes and a mocking demeanor who told me that I should inquire at the regional tourist office at the railway station. The young man there told me that La Tomatina was in fact only one part of a weeklong fiesta in honor of a saint, and that the tomato part was the result of a wedding that took place 31 years ago at which the guests forgot to eat the salad. They were too replete to eat it and too inebriated to be sensible, and so they threw it at one another. He told me that now the occasion actually begins with somebody climbing a pole to retrieve a ham, and I was reminded that in Portugal one does the same thing, except that there is a dried, salted cod at the top. He said that Buñol's population of 9,000 swells to 30,000 for La Tomatina, and don't wear any nice clothes, because it's traditional to have them ripped off you.

I soon learned that the history was not so clear; someone else told me that a cartload of tomatoes had overturned in the town about a hundred years ago and that, since the fruit was now spoiled, the people decided it would be fun to throw it at one another. The man in the newspaper shop said that in fact (and he should know— he has a relative there) it has always been traditional in Buñol for neighbors to throw things at one another during fiesta. Someone else told me that in truth La Tomatina arose out of a violent argument. What was agreed upon, however, was the fact that it had been banned under Franco, who, like all dictators, hated people to enjoy themselves. Apparently the Guardia Civil used to turn up to ensure that the fiesta was not happening, and then, after they had gone, the fiesta happened. Clearly, the "facts" about the fiesta were not forthcoming, so I decided to wait until I arrived in Buñol to separate myth from truth.

I left for Buñol at 8:00 a.m. on the day of La Tomatina. My train carried me at a sedate pace past an enormous necropolis, dark citrus groves, vineyards, fields of rich, red soil, and toward the breasted hills in which the town reclines. I was starting to feel apprehensive about my destination based on my observations of Valencian tomatoes, which are approximately the size of a baby's head. I was certain that someone would be killed. If this were England, there would be hooligans putting stones and razor blades inside the fruit. There was indeed an ominous message from the mayor in the festival program, which I'd picked up in Valencia: "We request that persons be respected; it is absolutely forbidden to bring glass bottles into the plaza, to destroy shirts, to annoy people with water bombs. Also we ask that tomatoes be squashed in the hand before they are thrown." I knew that it has always been the custom to throw *globos de agua* (balloons filled with water) at fiestas, and that in some South American countries the local thugs had taken to putting them in the freezer first. I began to worry about surviving intact.

I reached Buñol three hours before La Tomatina was scheduled to begin and made my way to the plaza that was to be the site of the event. The town is dominated by a large and ugly cement works and is divided by deep, jungly chasms containing tiny streams, carpeted and curtained in swaths of blue convolvulus. Prickly pears sprout with insouciance from the rocks, and the alleys between the houses consist of ramps and steps that form an unfathomable labyrinth, out of which there is no escape unless you single-mindedly decide to take any route that goes downward. To climb back up, you need iron lungs and the calf muscles of an Andean Inca.

It was clear when I arrived that people had already made preparations for the festivities: the houses along the only important street were draped with plastic sheeting. I planted myself in the middle of the tiny plaza and continued my study of the fiesta program. It revealed that the week's festivities were, most curiously, like any village fete in England, though much scaled-up and with greater emphasis upon bands and orchestras. Just as in Britain, there was a committee of efficient women in charge of the whole event, curious sports, fireworks, karaoke, football, a procession of carts, junior and senior fishing contests, a chess competition, a dog-obedience trial, tennis, cycling, and 24-hour ping-pong. In England we would have competitions for cake and jam and fruit rather than for *paella* and *gazpacho,* and we would place less emphasis upon religion. We might raise money by throwing wet sponges at the vicar, while in Buñol there are processions and offerings of fruit and flowers to St. Luis Beltrán and Our Lady of the Unprotected. Buñol is also superior in that it has not only a fiesta queen (this year it was Señorita María Eugenia Estepa Saez) but no fewer than fourteen beautiful and implacably wholesome maids of honor. I would have married all of them on the spot, either simultaneously or in sequence.

The plaza filled up slowly, and soon the whole street was packed in both directions, mainly with the youth of both sexes in about equal numbers but also with tiny children and intrepid representatives of older generations. Behind me two little boys filled a plastic bag with water from the public drinking fountain, swung it about their heads, and soaked me from head to foot. As it was again 104 degrees, I was profoundly grateful, and anyway I knew that I would be able to get them later. Next to me a group of friends began to tear one another's t-shirts. I moved away a little. A band of people with painted faces stretched banners across the street in order to protest a toxic-waste incinerator. A disabled man in a wheelchair passed by with a plastic bucket sensibly planted atop his head. A man in a bandanna ambushed a policeman and stole his badge. There ensued a good-natured scuffle, which the policeman won. The kids began to act up for the TV crews that were setting up in upper windows, where they thought that they would be safe. At

10:00 a.m. a man in a van appeared to hand out free wine from a barrel and complementary meaty pastries. For some reason the climbing of the pole to fetch the ham was canceled, and a group of young men paraded the pole through the street in protest. Three policemen tried to turn them back but then gave in.

It was now far too hot for those who were not in the shade, and they began to chant, "*Agua, agua, agua,*" to the two men and the woman standing on a platform just above our heads. So what if water bombs had been specifically forbidden? The people were begging to be soaked. There was a swift discussion, and then hoses were turned on the folk below, who clambered to get onto one another's shoulders in order to be better sprayed. They began to chant, "*Olé, olé, olé, olé, olé, olé.*" In Britain this is the favorite refrain of the more moronic variety of soccer fan, so I couldn't bring myself to join in, though it did remind me of *aioli*, which is a particularly nice garlic concoction from the south of France. Buckets of water began to be emptied on us from upper windows by kindly old gentlemen who in more glorious days would have been down below in the thick of the melee. They were acclaimed and begged to work faster. Sweatshirt and t-shirt tearing now became de rigueur, and the sodden rags were hurled high into the air, where they snagged on telephone wires and power lines and the wrought-ironwork of balconies. An Asian camera crew made the mistake of trying to film in the middle of the crowd. They had taken the precaution of covering their camera with plastic, but that didn't stop the Spaniards in their vicinity from pelting them with soaked morsels of clothing. They backed away with nowhere to go, holding up their hands for mercy, and the crowd began to chant again. At first I thought that we had been infiltrated by radical Socialists, because the new chorus had the same rhythm as "The people united will never be defeated." But no, they were chanting, "*Ea, ea, ea, el Chino se cabrea.*" I'm not sure, but I think that this means, "Hey, hey, hey the Chinaman's getting pissed off."

Friendly inhabitants turned hoses on us from the rooftops and were cheered and applauded. We were all hysterical with happiness before we had even seen a tomato. We began to chant, "*To-ma-tes,*

to-ma-tes, to-ma-tes," clapping on the first and last syllables; we
wanted tomatoes more than we wanted to be rich, more than we
wanted world peace, more than we wanted eternal youth. In Chiva
and Requena they probably heard us insisting upon tomatoes, and
in Venta Quemada I expect that tiles and chimneys toppled from
the roofs. It was like a striptease; the authorities were holding back
deliberately in order to stir up our excitement. *"To-ma-tes, to-ma-
tes..."* Our fists punched the air in unison, and it occurred to me
that this was what it must have been like at a Nuremberg rally. (If
only they had chanted *"tomates"* instead of *"Sieg heil."*)

Suddenly there was an explosion behind me that nearly caused
my soul to leave my body, and then a horn sounded far away. The
street's narrow and winding nature kept the vehicle's approach
hidden from view. Moments later, a huge dump truck was upon us,
its bed filled with tomatoes. On top of it were a dozen or so
tossers, who were hurling the truck's contents at us. Some of them
were wearing diving masks because they knew that we would just
throw the tomatoes back. I got a tomato thrown at full strength in
the nape of the neck and another in the chest. So much for being
the detached observer with a notebook.

The truck passed by, and I felt a little disappointed. It had been
fun, but it hadn't lasted long, and the tomatoes were already squashed
to a pulp.

Then another truck rolled through, and more fruit hurtled
down at us. Water continued to pour from the hoses above. What
had been a generous shower of tomatoes suddenly became an
alarming hailstorm. I tried to be clever and catch the ones that had
my number on them but very soon gave up. One tomato after
another crushed itself against every part of my anatomy, some with
a sharp stinging slap and others with a decadent and relaxed sper-
losh. I realized that there was absolutely not the slightest chance of
coming through unscathed, and I threw my Britannic reserve to
the winds. I knelt down and scooped tomatoes into my t-shirt; my
neighbors promptly pillaged them as I stood up, leaving me just
enough to practice mortar-bombing a fat man by a wall. How
much more satisfying it is when an accurate lob descends vertically

upon an unsuspecting soul than when one bowls a victim over with a baseball pitcher's velocity and ferocity.

There was another truck, and the alarming hailstorm transmogrified instantaneously into a red tornado. As the flurry of projectiles intensified, it became physically impossible for the senses to register details; individual tomatoes blurred into a whirling system of scarlet curves that crossed and cascaded. They flew with such rapidity that it was like watching the discarded straw flying from the back of a harvester. I grew wild-hearted and exhilarated.

Another truck sounded its horn, a deep blast like that of a ship in fog, and passed through the crowd. Our red tornado became an inexorable hurricane. It was becoming difficult to stand upright in so much slush and with so many wet missiles impacting from every possible direction. We blotted out the sun and sky with our remorseless fusillades and barrages. Water continued to sluice down upon us from roof and window. We staggered blindly with juice in our eyes and our feet spread wide for balance. When we caught one another's glances, it was with the complicitous and conspiratorial glee of mischievous children. Drenched in that stupendous slurry, we had abolished all distinctions of sex and age and country; we had achieved the extreme mutuality of a glorious and liberating madness.

There was another truck, and then I lost count. I was sliding and slipping, I was having a battle with a pair of twins, and I'd gone deaf in one ear because it was filled with pulp. I had peel up my nose, and my eyes were smarting painfully. I groveled ignominiously on the pavement, grabbing ammunition from the very hands of others. Somebody stuffed a handful of gloop down the front of my shorts. It was a fierce amazon who in daily life was undoubtedly dignified and sophisticated. I gave chase but lost her when I fell over. Somebody stood on me. I flung pulp backwards over my head, and they got off. Next to me an unfortunate middle-aged man was groping on his hands and knees for a shoe that he had lost beneath four inches of roseate splosh. I squashed a good two pounds on the heads of the two little boys who had soaked me earlier. I was now so completely drenched in juice that even my unmentionable parts began to sting horribly. My shoes were full; I had become one vast squelching mound of pulped tomato. A girl next to me burst into tears because someone had hurled a tomato into the side of her head at close range, and she was led away by a friend. I joined in the general effort to pelt the TV crews in the upper windows and balconies, and was in turn splatted by those behind me on the wall above the fountain. Semi-naked bodies in ripped and rended clothing whirled and wheeled and fought and collided. It was merciless; it was all against all without fear or favor. I could not recall ever having had so much fun.

The program said that at 1300 hours there would be a cleanup followed by a "*siesta popular,*" and accordingly there was another startling explosion at exactly one o'clock. To my amazement we all stopped fighting. I had assumed that we would be too far gone in hysteria and bacchanalian frenzy to obey any signal from the authorities, but the truth was that after an hour of total war we all were wholly exhausted. We stopped kicking slush at one another and returned to a normal state of consciousness, only to be astounded and amazed by the scene that we thousands had created among us. Anyone who has seen *Apocalypse Now* will remember the parts where everybody and everything is soaked in blood and gore. That is nothing compared with what we now beheld. The houses were splattered up to the roofs with tags of peel and flakes of flesh. Beneath us the street ran above our ankles with tomato puree. It was a sight from a slaughterhouse, a true picture of a prodigious biblical massacre, a benign catastrophe of epic scale.

People emerged with implements that looked like giant croupier's pushers and began to shove the copious pink slush down into the sewers. I took off my shirt and wrung a torrent from it. Some of us were helpfully hosed down by the folk who came out to clean their streets and houses, but somehow I missed out. And then there was a miracle, no doubt wrought by St. Luis Beltrán himself, a miracle that passed me by, I suppose, because I am not a Catholic. The crowd actually disappeared and then reappeared in sparkling clean clothes. I was dumbfounded. I was the only one left who was caked from bald crown to soggy shoelace in congealed fruit, and I was, as the Spanish saying goes, caught with my arse in the air.

I am used to feeling ridiculous (I have two sisters, after all), but I have never felt so shamefaced as I did when I discovered that I was the only one on the train back to Valencia who looked like an escapee from a charnel house, and the only one to wend his disheveled way back through the most public and chic part of Valencia under the superior gaze of café habitués who no doubt were remarking to one another, "He can't be a Catholic, he isn't clean, looks like the saint missed him. With shapeless shorts like that, he must be British."

I feared that I would not be allowed into the Hospederia Pilar in my hideous state, but a cleaning lady took pity on me and ran off to fetch my key. In my room I assessed the damage: camera full of juice, all body hair congealed with peel that had solidified in the heat, shoes full, socks hopelessly stiff and unremovable, white cotton underwear pink, notebook irretrievably dissolved, legs already aching to the point of agony. I suppose that in repeatedly gathering up ammo I must have done the equivalent of a couple hundred squats.

I left Spain deeply impressed by the Pantagruelian orgy in which I had taken part. Everything at La Tomatina happened exactly on time and just as planned—"a fabulous technical achievement on the part of the Red Cross, the Guardia Civil, and the local police," as one reporter put it. And this is odd when you consider that it was also the most consummate example of frenzied Spanish anarchy in which anyone could possibly wish to become embroiled.

It seems that a committee whose members are granted the honorific of "*tomatero*" provide the military efficiency and punctilious dedication that propel the event. The twelve *tomateros* have their own version of the fiesta's creation myth: they explain that it all began as a prank involving a salad at lunchtime one day in 1944, and profess themselves impressed by the way in which the festival now involves 10,000 people. Except that one of the papers says it was 20,000, and the man in the tourist office says it was 30,000.

Furthermore, the man at the newsstand says that in fact the tomatoes come from Extremadura, because the local tomatoes are too big and you cannot grow enough of them. He says that we threw 11,000 pounds. *Levante* states categorically that the tomatoes come from Cáceres and that there were 200,000 pounds, while *Las Provincias* says that it was 260,000 pounds. It was five truckloads, says the newsdealer; four truckloads, says *Levante*. All I know for sure is that it was certainly enough tomatoes to inundate half a mile of street to ankle depth and to keep 10,000 or 20,000 or 30,000 *franctireurs* gleefully slinging fruit for an entire hour, an hour that ended with all of us smiling inanely, our hearts full of a strange and inordinate affection for one another, replete with that conviviality so prophetically recommended by the mayor. "Let us create a collective climate of civility and urbanity which will substitute for the heat of summer the warmth of human cordiality," he had written in the program, and yes, we did a good job of that, if I do say so myself.

Let me work it out: I'm nearly 40, and I'll probably be too decrepit to participate by the time I'm 70. That means I can return to La Tomatina about 30 times. That might be enough, I suppose.

★

Louis de Bernieres has worked as a cowboy, a car mechanic, a landscape gardener, and a teacher of truants. His novel Corelli's Mandolin *was made into a movie starring Nicholas Cage and Penelope Cruz, and he is also the author of* Birds Without Wings.

BARBARA BANKS

✦ ✦ ✦

A Tibetan Picnic

As the belly fills, so fills the heart.

THE LAND CRUISER LABORS ITS WAY ACROSS THE COUNTRYSIDE, followed by the baby blue supply truck. We are in the remote stretches of Tibet to do field work, and it is two 16,000-foot passes since breakfast. Time is of little consequence in this immensity, and the decision to eat will be made by place, not by the clock. Open pasture stretches out on either side of the dirt road that passes for Tibet's major highway out here, and in the distance a girl is collecting yak dung in a basket to bring back to her village for fuel. Suddenly the Land Cruiser veers off the road and bumps across the sparse grass towards the river we have been following for hours, the blue truck lurching behind like a drunken dinosaur. We have arrived.

Dawa is out of the truck in moments, and climbs up the side bars to unlash the canvas top. He is a giant of a man, with a heart as huge as the sky and a wacky, Jackie Gleason sense of humor that can shake the road weariness out of us in moments. He reaches into the hold of the truck and drops three lumpy burlap sacks and the wooden tea churn to waiting arms below. Small fireplaces sprout across the grass like mushrooms, built of round stones packed with clay from the nearby river, and you realize why this spot was chosen above all the other promising sites you had passed, although how they could tell this or remember the distinguishing characteristics that mark this particular bend in the road remain a mystery, to be stored with many others that have filled your head since entering this beautiful enigma of a place. Phurbu the cook bends over the sticks and dried grasses he has gathered in one of the fireplaces, coaxing flames into life, and within moments the blackened tea kettle is set on the fire. Life does not continue without tea.

We are in a campsite used by countless people before us: nomads following their flocks down from summer pasture, traders walking their goods to the town that lies two days journey to the east, families making the long pilgrimage to Lhasa to honor the deities that protect their country. The sacks are untied; from one comes a full leg of a sheep. Refrigeration is both unavailable and redundant here; the dry air and the cold of the high plateau take care of it for you. From another sack a plump pillow of roasted barley flour and a large wooden bowl are pulled out, from the third a small rosewood bowl, its top tied with a leather lace. These are the ingredients for a Tibetan picnic.

We sit on the sun-warmed grass, sweaters around our shoulders against the promise of winter that haunts the wind. Shamba returns from the riverbank, his face and hands bright red from their scrubbing in the frigid water. He holds the tiny branch of a bare bush, which he sets down gently beside the teapot without saying a word, then joins our circle on the grass. Phurbu is kneading the barley with the first of the tea, working the flour around the edges of the bowl to make a dough. As each handful comes to the right consistency, he squeezes it in his fist and passes it to one of us, a tube of roasted grain imprinted with the mark of his sure hand. Dawa is at work on the leg of the sheep; he draws the dagger-like knife which every Tibetan man and most Tibetan women keep hanging from their waists for just such occasions. Everyone else pulls their daggers out as well; Dawa's is simply a big flattened steel bar, ground to an edge with a massive handle fitted on the end. We will make do with our Swiss Army knives, which look fragile as matchsticks in the company of all this serious metal. Dawa slices off chunks of mutton, throwing most of them onto the grass in the center of the circle; the irresistible chunks he pops directly into his mouth. When he has cut a good-sized heap he sets the leg down beside him. The rosewood bowl has been opened to reveal ground red pepper, which we tip into the lid as a serving bowl. There isn't a fork in sight, nor a plate or napkin for that matter. However, it is time to eat.

We fall onto the food as if it is the first we have seen in days, or the last we will see for days to come—and in truth you never know up here. Between bites of *tsampa*, the roasted barley flour dough, we reach into the pile of meat, dipping our pieces into the red pepper either on just one side or two, depending on how hot you like it. As the meat pile diminishes, the leg of mutton is passed around and we take turns cutting off more and throwing it into the pile, usually while we are both chewing and talking. Manners do count out here, but they are a different set of manners, and you get to break every rule that was drummed into you as a child. (This may be the real reason that people fall in love with Tibet.)

Meanwhile, Phurbu has poured the black tea into the wooden churn, and hooks his leg around it as a brace. He adds a knife-blade full of yak butter and a small handful of salt, then with the gesture that is rhythmic and graceful and practiced a thousand times over, he churns the *sö cha,* or butter tea, regular as a metronome. The tea is poured, thick as cream and the color of caramel, back into the black kettle, its smoky flavor interwoven with the scent of melted yak butter. Phurbu reaches over to the twig that Shamba had brought back from the river and fits it into the spout, a perfect strainer. Our cups are ready, always ready for tea: there are silver-lined traditional wooden tea bowls alongside plastic thermal mugs, and the

Yak

kettle is lifted time and again—no cup gets drunk to the bottom before being refilled, and the brothy mixture is warming from deep within. Here it is quite proper, expected even, that you will make a lot of noise when you eat. In fact, if you have no appetite but don't want to offend your hosts you can get by with a lot of smacking of your lips and swallowing sounds; they don't notice as long as you keep drinking your tea.

And so we sit, nine human beings in a circle, encircled by a wall of mountains that swallow up our laughter and tiny voices. We tell jokes and stories while we eat, tossing any unwanted bits over our shoulders until we are surrounded by a necklace of gristle and bone. Amidst the talk and jokes there is a sudden sharp crack. Dawa raises his dagger arm again and slices across the bone, taking the whole top off this time. For all their congeniality, Tibetan picnics can have a decidedly Neanderthal flavor to them. With the point of his ten-inch blade Dawa reaches into the bone for the marrow, eating it straight off the knife tip, the yellow sash swinging like a jaunty exclamation point from the handle. We wait our turn, knives ready.

Suddenly, without a spoken signal, the picnic ends. Burlap sacks are cinched closed and tossed back into the belly of the truck. Jackets are folded to once again provide seat cushions against the rutted road. The last of the tea is swung in an arc across the grass; the twig strainer is carefully removed from the spout and left by the fireplace for the next set of pilgrims. We pile into the vehicles and set off in silence, the spell of our meal together still hovering over that tiny spot in the immense Tibetan land.

⋆

Barbara Banks has been traveling since age five, when she ran away from home because her brother ate all of the ice cream. She has built wooden boats in France, driven a freight train across Turkey, and sailed across the North Sea. More conventional work has been as a documentary filmmaker and writer for an adventure travel company. She lives in Berkeley, California.

CHARLES N. BARNARD

Paper Patterns

In which Hong Kong fits like
a well-made suit.

THE STAR FERRY IS ONLY THREE MINUTES' WALK FROM THE
Mandarin hotel in Hong Kong, and although I would probably
never run for a commuter train in Connecticut, I am running now
through a crowded ferry terminal to catch the next boat, running
even faster than the scurrying Chinese, filled with an exhilaration
I can't explain at my age. Is it pure joy at being back in a place I
love? Or is it something else?

There is no real haste for me to cross the harbor at this moment—I'm going to be in Hong Kong for many days this time,
praise be—but a pulse of memory urges me to run the length of
the ferry pier as I did in the 1960s; to have the coins ready for the
turnstile; to race against the light that will turn red and the bell

Star Ferry

that will clang to announce that the gate is swinging shut; to squeeze past the gateman in his blue sailor suit and step aboard just as the man on the pier throws off the mooring hawser with that same weary skill I remember so well. In short, to be as quick now as when I was 39.

But it isn't just a race against getting older that I run; the calendar sets its own relentless pace, after all, and it never loses the birthday game. I run a different race. It is to stay ahead of change. If I'm quick enough, I say to myself, perhaps everything I love and remember will remain the same.

So today I run for the ferry.

It is often difficult for travelers to choose between the excitement of discovering new places and the bitter-sweet pleasures of going back to a favorite city, to memories and, yes, to changes. In a lifetime of travel the early years are the time for discovery. I will always remember my first astonished look at Hong Kong from the forward deck of the ferry. We were headed across the harbor from Kowloon to Victoria a quarter-century ago. A mass of tall white buildings was even then starting to creep up the green flanks of Hong Kong Island. I thought it the most exciting place I had ever seen.

Over the years I returned many times, and excitement turned to appreciation. Hong Kong and I matured together. Each time I came back, sometimes for only a few days, once for more than a month, I looked at my city as I look at my own face in a mirror. From year to year we didn't really change that much—did we?

Out of breath, I make the ferry. This one is *Celestial Star*. I wonder as I step onto the teak deck, How many times have I been on this same boat before? (And with whom as my companion?)

I used to be able to name all the Star Ferries. It was a recitation, a trivia catechism: "*Morning Star, Night Star, Day Star, Celestial Star, Twinkling Star, Shining Star, Solar Star, Meridian Star, Northern Star....*" (Love empowers memory; you keep what your heart wants to keep.)

Once aboard the venerable vessel, the sounds are all as I remember them: the engine room bells, the slosh of the propellers, the creaking groan of the ferry's rub rail against the timbers of the pier, the chatter of Cantonese, the hiss of spume flung against the side curtains by the chop.

Seven minutes later, on the Kowloon side of the harbor, I allow myself to be surged off *Celestial Star* by hundreds of determined Chinese in a hurry; and I follow yet another impulse. Why not go see George Chen again? His shop is just nearby. People say he is still the best tailor in Hong Kong. He made suits for me long ago when he was less famous. One was a gray tropical with a fine red pinstripe; I always liked that one.

In the best tailoring tradition, George had made paper patterns according to my measurements. He assured me that if ever I wanted a new suit, I could send my order from Connecticut and my patterns-on-file would guarantee a perfect fit.

It made me feel special in those days to know that a famous Chinese tailor 12,000 miles from home had "my patterns;" that just by writing a letter to him I could have a custom-made suit with all those little extra pockets and buttons and a wonderful, colorful silk lining.

As things turned out, I never did that. When the '70s arrived, that old devil Change dealt me a blow and there were many things I needed more than tailored clothes. There had been a divorce, a return to a city apartment, an attempt at a new career. A dry cleaner had ruined the gray tropical, and I gradually lost track of George Chen.

Now, years later, he looks exactly as I remember him, which pleases me. His new, larger shop, its walls stacked to the ceiling with bolts of fabric, looks much like the old one: same curtained fitting rooms, mirrors, fluorescent lights, and clutter of pins on the carpet. Eric Ng and Johnny Ho, the two apprentices I remember, have grown up, but not grown old. They say they remember me, which is polite, but I doubt that.

"We never forget an old customer," George says. "Come look at the file, you'll see why." His thin tailor's fingers walk over a tightly packed drawer of index cards. "Here you are: Barnard, C., Darien, Connecticut. Then you move to East Seventy-fifth Street. But where you go after that? It says, 'Christmas card returned, no for-warding address.'"

"I don't remember those years, George," I answer, remembering them all too well, "but I survived, I'm here now. What else does that little intelligence file of yours say about me?" (What do I want it to say? Happily remarried and back living in Connecticut again?)

"It says, 'Paper patterns on file,'" George reads with a smile. "And," he adds, tapping at my midsection with the backs of his fingers, "your figure hasn't changed so much."

Suddenly I know I am going to have a suit made. That wasn't the thought that brought me here, but now it seems an imperative, a way to win a round against change. The paper patterns, symbols of constancy, have done it.

"You wouldn't happen to have a gray tropical fabric with a fine red pinstripe, would you?"

"We'll find one!" says George, his face lighting up and looking very pleased. Without even a signal from the boss, Johnny Ho starts pulling down big bolts of fabric.

At this moment, it doesn't seem to matter a damn how old I am. It is 1965 again. All the unwanted changes of the years are suddenly erased. Hong Kong, like an old friend, has put its arm around my shoulders again. All is not lost.

That's what paper patterns are for, after all.

★

Charles N. Barnard has been roped to a Swiss mountain, gone scuba diving in Tahiti, played polo on elephant-back in Nepal, and learned to fly his own plane, all while roaming seven continents over the last fifty years. He is the managing editor of TravelClassics.com and has written for such publications as National Geographic Traveler, Smithsonian, Leisure, *and* Reader's Digest. *During his career he has been a senior editor at the* Saturday Evening Post, *editor-in-chief of* True, *and travel editor of* Modern Maturity. *He lives in Connecticut.*

JAMES O'REILLY

✶ ✶ ✶

Road Scholars

Eight thousand miles in France with three kids,
a van, and no hotel reservations.

OUR PLAN WAS TO SHIP OUR VW VAN—STUFFED AS THOUGH IT
were an indecently large suitcase—to France, drive around for six
weeks, find a town to our liking, and settle down for two years so
our three girls, aged three, five, and seven, could learn French while
I finished a book. Not exactly *A Year in Provence,* but maybe a year
or two in Montpellier, Pont-Aven, or Grenoble. Of course, it didn't
work out quite like that. Well, to be honest, it didn't work out like
that at all.

To begin with, there was the obligatory French dock strike. Our
van would be two weeks late, we were told, and it wasn't going to
arrive in France after all. Maybe Belgium, perhaps the Netherlands.
Normalement the boat would head for Antwerp after bypassing Le
Havre (where it was supposed to go), but for obscure reasons it
might have to unload in Rotterdam. Sitting on lumpy mattresses in
an atmospheric but squalid Left Bank hotel, Wenda and I took a
deep breath and decided to enjoy our fate while matters maritime
sorted themselves out.

We explored Paris, bitterly cold in early January but devoid of
tourists. There were no lines anywhere. The Eiffel Tower in a
rainstorm was ours. So too the Musée d'Orsay, the Louvre, and

Notre-Dame. There was nobody waiting for ice cream cones out-side Berthillon on l'Isle St-Louis. We were cheated by cab drivers and snubbed by waiters. We rode boats on the Seine, wandered the streets, visited Jacques Cousteau's Parc Océanique under Les Halles, spent exorbitant sums on mediocre snacks, and in general had a wonderful time. We decided Paris was indeed extraordinary, ooz-ing history and beauty like no other place, but that Parisians who deal with tourists bear a distinct behavioral resemblance to New Yorkers, Paris not being France the same way New York is not America. Or is it? The question had too many layers to sort out when a three-year-old wanted to be carried through all six million miles of the Louvre.

We rented a little red Peugeot, stuffed dolls, bears, and children into it and set off to find the real France, where we would set up shop. No sooner had we left Paris than one of the girls threw up all over the back seat. We pulled off the road next to a nice-look-ing *auberge* by the Seine and cleaned the car. By then everyone was hungry and cold, so we trotted past ducks and up stone steps and inquired if the establishment was open. It was, *bien sûr.* We were warmly welcomed, served great food at a reasonable price, and left feeling that perhaps we had not made a mistake after all, that in fact Parisians were only as good ambassadors as New Yorkers.

We headed for Normandy, where we stayed with friends in a farmhouse near Caen. We visited the Peace Museum, walked Sword Beach, and told the girls about World War II and the ap-proaching fleet had this been D-Day so many years ago. One evening I achieved *satori,* or, as Spalding Gray might have it, a per-fect moment, sharing wine and camembert with our friends. I am by no means a food-oriented person, but the French do indeed have a lovely and communicable way with food. The next evening, however, I made the mistake of expressing too much enthusiasm for *tripe à la mode de Caen* and needed to eat a lot to convince our hosts. In the morning my daughters entertained my sorry corpse with a dance they called "Let's Do the Cow Stomach."

In Villedieu-les-Poêles we visited a foundry where the church bells of France and other countries are made. We explored an empty, windswept Mont St-Michel and listened to organ practice in a chapel. One of the girls fell down a flight of stairs. A Mirage fighter roared overhead. The bay was magnificent, the solitude extraordinary.

We drove to Blois, on the Loire River, arriving late in the evening. By now the children had become night owls, but if we didn't feed them by eight, rebellion was at hand. We staggered into a full and too-expensive restaurant and asked if the chef could produce something for the children. He presented exquisite little steaks at a fraction of the cost of a Paris snack. Wenda and I rue-fully settled for shallow bowls of seafood soup, but after one mouthful it was apparent this was no ordinary soup. Many months later, in fact, on the Alaska Railroad, I struck up a conversation with one of the dining car waiters—he was French, from Blois—where he said there was a restaurant with this soup…How could soup be that good? I still wonder. But somehow it was.

We stayed in a hotel next to Château de Chambord, where we were fawned over by a staff who acted as though they hadn't had guests in years. In fact, we were the only guests. It had become clear to us that one of the merits of traveling in winter with chil-dren was that hotel and restaurant staffs were more indulgent—and forgiving—than they might have been at peak season. But apart from the pros and cons of winter travel, we found people all over France to be warm and caring, especially toward children. Wherever we went, people seemed to look out for our daughters. It felt safe to let them out of our sight in a way that it doesn't in America.

In the morning, we explored the Château and its extraordinary ramparts and double-helix staircase. Huge fires blazed in the fire-places, but couldn't chase the chill. I scattered a friend's ashes on the frozen Cosson River nearby; when spring came, he'd be carried into the Loire.

That night we walked the perimeter of Chambord, vast, dark, mysterious, Orion bright and hard in the January sky. We heard the laughter of the Château's guardians floating from their living quarters, mocking the excess of the dead.

We headed south, past the sprawl of Lyon, to a walled farmhouse high over vineyards near Orange in northern Provence. The mistral howled all night but we slept well, aided by our hosts' own wine.

By now we had seen dozens of towns and were adept at squeezing the car late at night down alleys meant for people and horses, in search of shelter. But a disturbing theme began to appear—we liked many places, but we couldn't see ourselves living in them. "Let's check out the next town," became our theme. The girls protested, but by now they were beginning to qualify as Road Warriors, if not Road Scholars yet. When they tired of history lessons, we reminded them they could be at school back in the States instead of eating chocolate for lunch and driving around France. Life could be worse. We told ourselves the same thing, but the fact is, we were getting worried. Little did we know we would be doing the same thing four months and thousands of miles later.

We thought we'd like Aix-en-Provence, but there were an alarming number of tollbooths straddling the *autoroute* outside of town warning of the hordes to come once the weather turned warm. We drove around for an hour before finding a parking spot and then stepped out into a pile of dog *merde,* and were immediately panhandled. These incidents, we decided, did not constitute good omens, and after looking around the admittedly lovely city, we decided it would be a great place to live in as a student, but that it was too crowded for us. So it was back to the road.

Near Bordeaux, we stayed on a farm where the girls saw hoursold baby goats and drank fresh warm goat's milk. Later, on another farm, they made butter with the farmer's wife and mother and saw a calf still steaming from birth. These farm experiences came to be an important part of the Road Scholar Curriculum, along with almost daily tutoring from Wenda.

We hastened on, for it was time to pick up our van, which we had been told was in Belgium. We dropped by our friends' Normandy home to recuperate, and then headed back to Paris. We stayed in a miserable hotel and took the train to Antwerp the following misty grey morning.

On the way to the shipping office, we had a cab driver who spoke French, Dutch, Flemish, German, and English. By now I think the utility of multilingualism was beginning to sink into the girls' minds and their games had a mixture of French and pretend French. They could see how ineffective I was with only minimal French, but how well their mother—fluent in French and Italian—could communicate. To be monolingual is to be socially hobbled, no matter how much of the world speaks English. The next morning, Wenda asked them if they wanted to wash their hair, and the three responses were, "Oui, bien sûr," "Weird, bien sûr," and "Oui, bien sure."

We drove through stack after towering stack of sea-freight containers until we arrived at one which mercifully contained our van and manifold contents. The children were delighted to renew acquaintance with toys and clothes; we were astounded at the quantity of stuff we'd thrown at the last minute into our capacious van, so full that if we parked on an incline and opened the door, goods to stock a Wal-Mart tumbled out.

We sallied forth again, crossing Belgium and Luxembourg to the Alps and Chamonix, where we were to meet friends for a week of skiing near Mt. Blanc. Our often-prescient oldest daughter suggested that this was the town we should live in. The people were friendly, it was the right size, and even though there were tourists, the outlying villages were appealing. But adults are a thick-headed lot, and we said no, there were other places more appropriate (sniff) than a ski town. We crossed the Massif Central, visited Lourdes in its exquisite Pyrenean setting, congratulating ourselves that we didn't buy even one ashtray of the Virgin, saw vineyards covered in snow, drove through innumerable hamlets that charmed but didn't hold us.

The fact is, we were on a driving jag. The *autoroutes* were empty, the hotels still empty, the prices off-season low, and the children were seeing more of France than many French do in a lifetime. We completed our second circuit of the country and drove into Switzerland. In Geneva, the girls watched a friend work the floor of the U.N., lobbying on behalf of Tibet. We drove to Lausanne with its Transport Museum, Vevey and its Alimentarium, Interlaken, Zurich, and into Austria. But much as we enjoyed everything, we were happy to leave highway *ausfahrts* behind and return to French *sorties*. At least we were in the right country, learning about France and the French if not much French itself.

By now we had hit upon our best tactic for ensuring the girls' cooperation in exploring historic and religious sites—we bought postcards before entering and had the kids look for what was on the cards. It was also becoming clear to us, the more we roamed, that parents too routinely surrender the job of teaching to schools. There is great joy in seeing how your children learn, in a way you can't when you just help with homework at night. We also gained renewed respect for the work teachers do.

Heading south again, we committed cultural heresy by visiting EuroDisney, feeling it was small payback for months of good behavior in the back of the van. Nonetheless, to make up for our sins we hastened to Versailles. In the vast cobbled courtyard, my oldest daughter took me aback by pointing at the palace and asking "Daddy, can we buy one of those?" Their favored mode of viewing the Sun King's treasures was to lie on the floor and study the splendid, intricate ceilings.

On our third Tour de France now, we thought seriously about settling in Pont-Aven, the lovely town in Brittany where Paul Gauguin once lived, but a bizarre April Fool's day encounter with a potential and emotionally disturbed landlord, replete with symbolism that would have us laughing later—a huge spider in a closet, mold, a rainy funeral, a dead horse, deviation road signs, and the fact that I was reading Stephen King's *Dead Zone*—sent us back to the *autoroute* with a sigh of relief.

But by now we had been driving for more than four months with only a week's letup here and there in a *gîte* (a country place for rent), and everyone's nerves were fraying. One night our three-year old shouted in a restaurant at the top of her lungs, "I hate menus! Just bring me food!" We, slow-to-learn grownups, began to wonder—perhaps we were overdoing this.

We went back to Normandy and left our van in a barn surrounded by chickens and bales of hay, and took the train to Paris.

We rented an apartment for a week, an expensive proposition at first blush, but cost-effective for a family when you consider meals not eaten in restaurants. Our place was directly across the Seine from Notre-Dame Cathedral, which filled our living room windows, and around the corner from what was then Mitterand's Left Bank home.

One night, *Vertigo,* Hitchcock's evocative San Francisco masterpiece, was on TV, and I discovered I could watch it in the dining room mirror with Notre-Dame also reflected there. A heady combination of wonders sent my head spinning, places and names scrolling before my eyes: Pont Neuf, North Beach, Pont-Aven, Mission San Juan Bautista, Pont d'Avignon, and Jimmy Stewart and Kim Novak struggling under the Golden Gate Bridge!

It was time to go.

Although we never did find a home on that first trip, we've since returned to France. And of course, my daughter was right. We returned to a village in the Haute-Savoie a few kilometers from Chamonix, where she and her sisters are in a public school. PE includes instruction in downhill and cross-country skiing and they are now correcting their mother's pronunciation. Mine, they just laugh at.

✳

James O'Reilly, president and publisher of Travelers' Tales, wrote mystery serials before becoming a travel writer in the early 1980s. He's visited more than forty countries, along the way meditating with monks in Tibet, participating in West African voodoo rituals, and hanging out the laundry with nuns in Florence. He travels extensively with his wife Wenda and their three daughters.

MORITZ THOMSEN

Tambourine Men
of Recife

*The music they produce reveals something
profound and true to those who listen.*

RECIFE. OK. I WILL WALK ACROSS TOWN AND LOOK FOR A REEF.
The town's harbor, lined with rusty freighters and incredibly old
coastal steamers, is like a wide river with the reef, now covered in
a long, thin line with huge rock chunks, forming the river's far
bank. The ocean breakers crashing against this long stone wall
throw up spray that shines in the sun where isolated figures of boys
in swimming trunks with long cane poles throw lines into the surf.
Their poses as they wait are as languorous and studied as Whistler
drawings. Everything, even the distant boys, the boats, the docks,
the street deep in the shade of mangos, the piled rocks at the reef,
has a timeless, frozen look. Something planned by Englishmen,
something built to last, a memorial to a decent past, that old vanished world of my grandfather's "where a man's word is his bond."

This section of town where the sailors hang out is a barrio of
neglected and seedy one-storied buildings, narrow streets, and old
trees. In a way it reminds one of San Francisco's Haight-Ashbury
district during the '60s, a place that reflects the passions and vices of
another time. The bars are as menacing as opium dens; no movie
set could capture the sense of danger and violence that these
façades suggest. Looking into their dark entranceways one is sur-

prised at the quiet (it is early afternoon) when one is straining to hear the shrieks of drunken syphilitics in various stages of delirium tremens or the whistle of knives being thrown into careless backs. The skid row section of Recife, what a setting for the last chapter of a sordid novel about moral disintegration. In the last century, Joseph Conrad's bars, by comparison, are as classy as the Raffles Hotel; not even Jim in his moments of most intense self-loathing would have pushed against these swinging doors from which the paint has peeled off in blisters as though boiled away by the heat of the passions and vices inside.

Close to the river some parallel streets have been closed to car traffic. All day and at night until midnight people stroll along these malls or sit on benches enjoying the coolness. There is a flower market at one end of one street, great piles of fruit massed at the other end; when seen from a block away even at night the pure glowing colors—orange, scarlet, apple red, the yellow of marigolds or daisies—are celebrations, great shouts of joy. Hucksters, magicians, kids, or older men or women with trays of cheap jewelry or razor blades or Japanese cassette tapes wander back and forth with small expectations. At ten o'clock at night comes a religious procession of priests and acolytes, and behind them heavy, soberly dressed women all with candles that illuminate the tragic faces they have assumed for the occasion, and behind them people off the street who fall in at the rear until the street is more procession than onlookers. Everyone is singing; everyone is solemn. It is 16th century; very heavy-duty stuff. It is intensely moving to be in a city where *everyone* believes in God, and I consider joining them, not because I believe in God, but because, though the spectacle is depressing for its ritual, I believe in the emotion that has joined them together.

One night, bored with sitting in the park just outside the hotel and bored with establishing half-comical, half-grotesque father-daughter relationships with whores, I wander into the mall, drawn there by the sound of music. On one corner at the center of a small crowd two men are singing songs of their own invention: a highly stylized dialogue between friends, a friendly argument, the purest, most authentic music I have ever heard. The singers are two brothers in their late twenties. The older, one leg shorter than the other, walks with a terrible swooping stagger. They are poorly dressed in stained t-shirts and stiff, cheap trousers. An older man is working with them, an old confidence man in a double-breasted coat, spotty and rumpled, that is many sizes too large for him. His face has the blank, corrupted look of a man who has fooled too many people with cheap tricks. His younger companions also have a blankness growing in their faces, a pitilessness as though they have begun to withdraw from a life that has lost its promise and its challenge. The three of them hold tambourines, and at the end of each verse they tap and shake them in a most subtle and controlled way, drawing from these simple clown's instruments the most precise and delicate sounds.

Each brother sings one verse to the other. I cannot understand the words except for the first sentence of each verse. *"Hermano, tu no sabes nada."* Each one emphasizes the last word, *nada*, in a way that is strong, innocent, and loving and then goes on to comment, correct, expand, or digress. "Brother, you don't understand how things are." The crowd is controlled absolutely by the singers, even the cops, who are mentioned from time to time in satiric ways. The people laugh, sigh, nod their heads wisely, or look vaguely at the ground as though great truths were being revealed to them by this simple and profound music that is coming to them from out of the heart of a great country. This is music out of the *sertão*, music made of dust, sticks, rocks, fickle women, mean storekeepers, fate, death, sun.

I listen for twenty minutes, for half an hour, keeping tight control of myself to not break into tears, to keep from dancing, embracing the singers, taking out all my money and laying it at their feet. In some sense that I don't understand, it is the most overpowering music I have ever heard; I want to sob, laugh, clap, and jump around; I want to shake one of the listeners, an old man, who seems unaffected, and yell at him, "But listen, listen, this is incredible."

As they sing, as they lose themselves in the music, their faces beam, transfigured. They are radiant with a pleasure that comes from doing something with flawless skill. It is possible, though I don't notice, that our own faces have changed and now reflect a profound delight, one of the best pleasures in the world: the joy in watching men who are doing something at which they excel.

If there is a sadness in watching the singers, it is one that is grounded in my American sense of values. It is sad to watch great artists wasting their sweetness. They are too great for the streets of Recife; there is an incongruity in their rags and in this little crowd of twenty that is gathered around them rather than at the amphitheater that would hold the thousands they deserve. I would not travel to Madrid to stand before some single Bosch in the Prado, but perhaps one day I will go back to Recife and wander the malls listening for the tapping sound of those tambourines, the glittering sound of those tambourines like a gush of water and those pure, plain voices revealing something profound and true about Brazil.

When the concert is over I give the older man a one hundred cruzeiro bill; he accepts it nicely, modestly proud that someone has recognized the true power of their art. And every night for the four nights more that I stay in Recife, I go out into the mall after dinner and stand in the crowd, stunned by the emotion that the three men create in those country songs that transform their faces and that open up life to those of us who listen.

*

The late Moritz Thomsen, born in 1915, made his home for many years in Guayaquil, Ecuador. His first book, Living Poor, *chronicles his four-year Peace Corps experience of living in a small fishing village in Ecuador in the 1960s. He returned to Ecuador after leaving the Peace Corps to become a farmer on the Rio Esmeraldas, an experience he describes in* The Farm on the River of Emeralds. *He also wrote* The Saddest Pleasure: A Journey on Two Rivers, *from which this story was excerpted. He continued to travel and live in South America until his death in 1991.*

JON CARROLL

* * *

The Great Invisible
Pheasant Hunt

It's the manly thing to do.

WE WERE STAYING IN A CRUMBLING PALACE IN THE TOWN OF M——,
in the arid western region of India called Rajasthan. We were guests
of the maharajah's son and his wife.

We had arrived there, rogue journalists on a tour of odd back-
waters, because there was some thought that the maharajah's son
might turn the palace into a hotel. He was, quite frankly, strapped
for cash—not like the glorious past, when hereditary feudal rulers
could levy taxes whenever they felt like it. Those were the bad old
days, unless you happened to be a maharajah.

The maharajah's son and his wife were about the same age as
my wife and I. We were all four of us talkative; we were all curious. He poured whiskey after whiskey; we talked and we talked.
Dinner receded infinitely. At around 9:30, we began dropping
hints, but it was not until midnight that we actually sat down to
solid food.

During the course of this marathon chat session, the maharajah's
son asked me if I wanted to go pheasant hunting the next day.

"Of course," I said boisterously. I had never hunted a pheasant,
or indeed anything at all, in my life.

"Wonderful!" he said. "I shall await you at 6:30!" I believe we toasted each other at that point. It was a jolly moment of cross-cultural camaraderie.

The next morning was not quite so jolly. I was up and dressed and bright-eyed and nauseated at 6:30; I sat in the big room ("living" room? I have no idea) and waited for my host to arrive. I pictured him in jodhpurs—we were not that far from the actual city of Jodhpur.

But there was only silence in the great palace. Not a creature was stirring, not even a scion.

I went ambling down the empty halls. "Hello?" I called. "Hello?" There was only silence. I came upon courtyards that I had not noticed before; I surprised elderly women beating wet clothing with rocks.

"Hello," I said. They drew back in horror.

I wanted more than anything to go back to bed. I wanted more than anything to take this deep silence throughout the palace as a sign. I wanted to delay as long as possible the actual hunting of the pheasant.

My experience with guns was limited to a .22 (target practice as a youth, for increased manliness) and an M-1 (ROTC as a youth, to increase our nation's readiness to meet aggression). The idea of taking whatever weapon was handed me and blasting away at a blameless bird…what could I have been thinking?

But I did not wish to disgrace myself. I did not wish to let our side down. Perhaps he meant to meet me at the front portico, or at the garage, or in yet another courtyard. So I wandered, head pounding, fear clutching at my gut. "Hello?"

Finally came the answering call. I stood stock still. It came again. I answered. After a minute, the maharajah's son appeared at the head of the staircase. He was in sleeping attire. His hair was mussed. He was scratching his head.

"I thought of the hunting to the pheasant we were have been going to go an hour ago," I remarked, inventing a new tense, the past perfect humiliative.

"Right you are," he said. "Right you are." Still he stood there. "Right you are. I'll just…"

"By all means," I said. "I'm fine."

He went away and I went back to the big room. I sat in an overstuffed chair and read one of those British magazines featuring stout women holding stout chrysanthemums. Time passed slowly. I began dreaming of antacid tablets.

He appeared at the door, dressed and vigorous. "Right then. Early start. Best thing. Shotgun all right?"

"Shotgun would be splendid," I said. We were both lying through our teeth.

So I was experiencing serious breakfast deprivation, and my head hurt just a little, and the Jeep was bouncing along a severely rutted road, and there was a shotgun with my name on it somewhere in the back.

Next to me was the maharajah's son. We were in Rajasthan, a part of India that looks a lot like Palmdale. Some of Rajasthan has the stark, desolate beauty of the great deserts of the world, but we were not in that part.

We were in the scrubby, bumpy, dotted-with-stunted-trees, already-too-hot-at-nine-in-the-morning part. We were off to shoot some pheasant. It was not something that either of us wanted to be doing, but we were doing it anyway. Such is the grave courtesy of our two great nations!

We reached a spot where someone had once seen a pheasant. The maharajah's son and I got out of the Jeep. He handed me the shotgun. It was the first shotgun I had ever held. Fortunately, I am an American; I knew how to hold it without looking stupid.

I was going to be fine, I knew, until it came time to fire it. But after that... I began obsessing about the "kick." I knew that average citizens were always surprised by how much recoil a weapon has. "It's not like in the movies," they would stereotypically remark, while being treated for a dislocated shoulder.

"Fine day for a hunt," said the maharajah's son.

"Fine, fine day," I said. My mouth twisted upward.

Some men were sent out to belabor the bushes. They were the "beaters" (I knew this from mystery stories); their job was to flush a startled pheasant from its lair. Then we would merrily blast away at the damn thing. That was the plan.

The men disappeared over the lumpy horizon. We could hear their patented pheasant-frightening calls. "Woo-eee," came the ghostly cries. "Woo-eee."

We stood there with our weapons. A bead of sweat ran down my cheek. We stood there and stood there. The choir invisible continued to frighten putative pheasants in the distance.

Finally, the men reappeared. One waved his hands and shouted in a foreign tongue. "Good, they've got one," said the maharajah's son. We peered into the scrub before us. It was silent and still; not a leaf moved.

"There it is!" he yelled.

I peered more deeply into the underbrush. I saw nothing. "Where?" I asked.

The maharajah's son pointed. "Just by that big yellow rock. You can see the feathers." Still, I saw nothing.

"Oh, yes," I said confidently.

"Your shot, then. Quickly now." Swell. I put the shotgun to my shoulder. I wondered about the state of orthopedic surgery in rural India. I fired in the direction of the yellow rock.

"Splendid. You've winged him." He called out to the beaters. They loped purposively off down a gully. "Fine shot," said my host.

"And the gun didn't really hurt my shoulder," I said. He looked at me curiously. Probably that's not a sentiment that pheasant hunters share with each other.

The beaters returned fifteen minutes later. They could not locate the wounded pheasant. "Bad luck," said the maharajah's son.

"Perhaps you'll score a clean kill," I suggested. I was swaggering just a bit—wounded bird, intact shoulder, manly chat with demi-royalty.

"I think not," said the maharajah's son. "Hot day today. I'd enjoy a whole day of sport, but duty calls. Duty calls."

It was the graceful way out. An expedition desired by no one had concluded with the imaginary wounding of an invisible bird. We had successfully agreed to tell the same lie, which is the essence of courtesy.

*

Jon Carroll writes a daily column for the San Francisco Chronicle.

* * *

Glide and the Family Church

This is one church where even the
intolerant are made whole.

I KNEW THIS WAS NOT GOING TO BE A NORMAL DAY AT CHURCH when I encountered a tall transvestite in the bathroom. He was preening over the sink—the sink that I wanted to use. What should I do? If I waited maybe he would think I was interested in him. I could always say something like, "Could you please get the hell out of here—you make me uncomfortable." Or maybe just, "Excuse me" would do. I opted for a hasty retreat as he adjusted the fur cap on his head. I thought as I was leaving, "That was stupid, the poor guy didn't do anything to you." Nonetheless, I was relieved to join the congregation through the side door as I weaved my way through rich and poor alike.

I sat down and immersed myself in the atmosphere of expectation. Voices muted, laughter and greetings hinted at—Sunday cleanliness evident—it was definitely a Sunday crowd. What was different was the altar. There was no altar; instead there was a band setting up and the Sunday atmosphere was clarified by the overwhelming perception that I was at the theater. Three chatty lesbians sat down in front of me and a blonde with a punk haircut and a face that had seen too much of the world sat next to me. There were families with children and gay men holding hands, all mixed in with old people who were spiritual misfits or diehard leftists, yuppies seeking an inner city experience, and your average, wide-open San Francisco types of all ages. "My," I thought, "what an interesting crowd." We were all—gay, straight, crooked, and broken—waiting for the show to begin. Outside at Ellis and Taylor, the derelicts and homeless had gathered to be part of the show in their own way. They would wait for the crowds to come out of church to ask for change; beggars at the banquet, they could be counted on for color.

The music started, heavy on gospel harmonies, the lights went on and the choir started to dance and sing its way out of the back staging area. There was no cross on the stage where there used to be an altar of some sort, only a blank, curved wall twenty feet high where images from a slide projector could be seen flickering like a throwback to a 1960s dance hall.

"Praise God, here we go," I thought to myself, "the party begins." As the singing got louder and the choir emerged fully on stage, the audience jumped out of their seats and joined in, clapping hands to the powerful rhythms. The Reverend Cecil Williams walked slowly onto the stage and told us in deep and persuading tones that no one would remain dead in his church, that Glide was a church where people came *alive*. The band and the choir filled the church with praise—all of us caught up in clapping our hands and shaking to the beat—while images of soulful children and struggling women appeared on the wall. The montages of the '60s were all there on the screen and in the audience. I wouldn't have been the least bit surprised if Janis Joplin herself had jumped on stage and launched into one of her hard-core rhythms about needing a man to understand her. Vague images of Bill Graham's Winterland Arena came to mind as I watched Reverend Cecil gazing upon the crowd with a faintly avuncular air. Strobe lights flashed and the ghosts of dead rock stars seemed to haunt the hall as the music rolled in waves through the church.

Indeed, whether it embodies worship or just a good time, Glide fills a need people have to come together and get sociable with God. This is different from the regular worship I am used to but I suspect that God enjoys all of it. The Master of galaxies and semen, oceans and dung, fools and sharks, God probably gets a bit tired of those ministers who think he is just some kind of power food. Add grace and stir—none of that stuff here.

The Reverend Cecil smoothly insinuated himself between the music and the crowd to take charge of the collective vibration that is the Glide Memorial experience. We were, he said, to express ourselves, as at Glide there would be no uninvolvement. I loved the heavy emphasis he gave to words like *involvement* and *commitment*. He said them as if they were more than mere words. Coming from his lips they were like some kind of psychic syrup designed to catch souls. I couldn't help but think that my young boys (the oldest is four) would find this kind of church very much to their liking. They would be able to jump around and shout and dance and participate in a way that is not the norm at our family's Catholic church in Arizona.

We were encouraged to hug the person next to us. This is a great place to hug someone of a different sexual persuasion than yourself. I took great pleasure in hugging lesbians and gays, a kind of contrarian perversion if you will. More singers were introduced. There were solos, some good, some not so good. Despite the exotic mix of people who come to Sunday service, Glide is still an inner city church with a black gospel feel.

Reverend Cecil got up—he had been sitting—and announced that there would be no sermon as he had a special guest who would be giving her own sermon. He gave some more glowing introductions and then said, "Would you please welcome Maya Angelou." The crowd leapt to its feet as if a rock star had just been announced. The choir could hardly control its emotion. Faces radiated wonder and excitement. Lesbians gazed with reverence at Dr. Angelou and wackos of all sorts acted as if a saint was in their midst. So went my thinking.

Ah, but how surprised I was when Maya opened her mouth to do her rendition of "This Little Light of Mine." "Hey," I thought, "this woman is *good*." Maya Angelou is a wave rider except she doesn't ride waves, she rides words. I felt what she felt, got what she got—in short, I was moved. Here I am, perhaps a tad to the right of Newt Gingrich, and I am digging Bill Clinton's Poet Laureate. Perhaps hell had frozen over while I wasn't looking, perhaps I had expired and people were stepping over my dead body while pigs flew overhead in formation. Thoughts of a more irreverent nature towards the President began to fill my atavistic mind. Sorry, I am in church, I should behave. Improper and vile thoughts sometimes slip by. Certainly lewd ones are the music in my elevator. But what would Reverend Cecil say? I should be ashamed.

As I was engaged in my usual diatribe with myself, a petite Asian woman pushing the limits of respectability in a short black dress and power hairdo walked onto the stage. I was intrigued. Who was this? Reverend Cecil said, "I would like to introduce my wife, she is going to go over the calendar and update you on the church's activities." His wife seemed to be champing at the bit; when she opened her mouth I knew why. This woman had something to say in a big way. Within minutes I had heard how high school dropout ratios had gone down and truancy statistics had dropped by 30 percent in the parish's area. She lectured us, she admonished her husband in front of the crowd, they flirted with argument, they bantered (Reverend Cecil was enjoying this), she hit us over the head with statistics, such as Glide having 35 comprehensive programs for over 500 children. I knew then that I was in the presence of the Empress of the Tenderloin. "How San Francisco of them," I thought, "blacks and Asians working together. What a combination." I later found out that the lady in question, Janice Mirikitani, had been held in a Japanese internment camp as a child in Arkansas, is a survivor of child abuse, and has been with Glide for 30 years. She is a Sansei (third-generation Japanese American) an author, poet, dancer, choreographer, and former high school teacher.

As I listened to this remarkable Japanese American president and executive director of Glide, with the choir behind her like a rainbow honor guard, I felt a window open onto the past. William Leidesdorff, Mammy Pleasant, and A Toy; the names roll off the tongue with a certain melancholy. The black sailing captain and builder of San Francisco's first city hall, black madam-cum-businesswoman extraordinaire, and the Chinese madam's madam; they were among the more colorful characters out of San Francisco's past. There, thumping with the beat of the band in the ruins of Christianity, was old San Francisco.

I shook my head as the service ended and headed quickly for the door. I had to make the 12:00 Mass at St. Cecilia's.

★

Sean O'Reilly is director of special sales and editor-at-large for Travelers' Tales. He is a former seminarian, stockbroker, and prison instructor with a degree in Psychology. Author of the controversial book on men's behavior, How to Manage Your DICK, *he is also the inventor of a safety device known as Johnny Upright. A life-long devotee of good humor and all things sacred and profane, his recent editorial credits include:* Travelers' Tales China, The Best Travelers' Tales 2004, Hyenas Laughed at Me and Now I Know Why, Travelers' Tales American Southwest, Travelers' Tales Ireland, Travelers' Tales Grand Canyon, Danger!, The Ultimate Journey, *and* Testosterone Planet. *Widely traveled, Sean most recently completed a journey through China and Southeast Asia. He lives in Virginia with his wife and six children.*

ARTHUR DAWSON

⋆ ⋆ ⋆

Police Beat

*A couple's run-in with the law reveals
a surprising code of enforcement.*

WITH OUR MONEY RUNNING OUT AND OUR BRAZILIAN VISAS
expired for well over a month, Jill and I walked into the headquar-
ters of the Policia Federal in the coastal town of Maceió. Presenting ourselves to the green-uniformed policeman at the front desk,
we explained our situation. He pushed some buttons on a grey mechanical adding machine, then pulled back a lever to get the total.

"Your fine will be three million *cruzeiros*," he announced. The
amount was almost double what we'd expected, a quarter of our
slim assets.

"But," I protested, "the police in Rio said it would be less than
two million."

"Yes, but because of inflation the fine has just increased to fifty-
six thousand *cruzeiros* a day."

I started to tell him we didn't have much money, but his attention had shifted to Jill, who had tears streaming down her cheeks.
Drawn by this display of feminine distress, another officer appeared
from the back of the office. The two officials conferred in a blur of
Portuguese and quickly reached a decision.

"It may be possible that you only pay a portion of your fine....
Or you could pay when you come back to Brazil," they said,

anxiously studying Jill's face to see if their words were having any effect.

"Could we really?" she asked, not quite believing it.

"Yes, yes," one of them replied, sounding more decisive.

"That would be good," she said, drying her eyes.

Relieved, the policemen dropped their shoulders. "Come back after lunch and we'll take care of it."

Returning that afternoon, we were directed to a pair of chairs facing a desk presided over by a man in his twenties, who wore a white shirt rather than a uniform. "My name is Pedro Wanderly Vizu," he said in excellent English, grasping our hands warmly and gesturing for us to have a seat. As he pulled official forms from several drawers and file cabinets, piling an impressive stack of paperwork on his desk, I wondered if Pedro might be annoyed with all the work we'd created for him, but his attitude remained light-hearted and friendly.

"Tell me why you did not leave Brazil," he asked, feeding a document into his typewriter.

"Because we like it too much!" said Jill, and all three of us burst out laughing. Getting more serious, the two of us described the events of the past month, while Pedro faithfully recorded them on the form. It was enough to fill a small novel: our desire to stay for Carnaval (any Brazilian would be sympathetic to this); our attempts to find cheap passage to Africa, and finally, how we were booked on a flight to Luxembourg, leaving in seven days.

"May I see your air ticket receipts?" Pedro asked.

Digging out the slip of paper, Jill handed it over. I was curious to see what Pedro's reaction would be when he saw our tickets had cost thirty-seven million *cruzeiros*, many times the penalty we owed. His only comment was, "If I saved for thirty years I could fly to Europe, look around for ten minutes, and then I'd have to return to Brazil."

The two of us sat quietly as he typed our story in quadruplicate—the office lacked both a copy machine and carbon paper. I was amused by the subtle irony of our situation—here we were, two Americans going into debt to Brazil, one of the biggest debtor nations in the world, much of it owed to the United States. Too bad Brazil couldn't subtract our fine from its financial obligations.

The typewriter paused its clattering as Pedro fed it another form. "What is your address in Maceió?" he asked.

"Green tent, *sem numero*, Riacho Doce Beach," I answered.

Pedro chuckled as he typed it in. "*Sem numero*" or "without number," is a common address in Brazil, where many buildings are unmarked. Checking off a box near the bottom of the document, he marked our status as one step short of "*Deportação*."

Noticing a guitar leaning against the windowsill behind Pedro's chair, I asked if he played.

"A little. Do you?"

I nodded.

After a couple of hours of tedious form-filling, broken frequently by off-the-record jokes and conversation, Pedro rose from his chair and led us to another police station a few blocks away, where the local constable took our fingerprints.

"If you were being deported they would have taken your picture also," Pedro informed us with a grin.

On the way back to his office, Jill asked, "What happens when we come back to Brazil? Are they going to make us pay the fine before we can enter the country?"

"Oh, no," Pedro replied. "You can enter with no problem. You will have to go to a Federal Police station to pay it."

"Will they know how much our fine is?"

"Oh no. You'll have to tell them how much it is." After a short silence, he announced, "Since you cannot pay your fine, you will have to play a song when we get back to the station."

Back at his desk, Pedro stapled our fingerprints to one of the forms and had us sign every document—I lost count after the twelfth one. Pedro and three of his office mates put their signatures below ours; every form had to have four witnesses.

When all the dotted lines were full, we opened our passports and received special exit visas stamped in purple ink. If we weren't out of the country in eight days, we'd be shipped by bus to Venezuela.

"It's time to pay your fine," Pedro said. Picking up his guitar, he led us to the door of the police chief's office. Putting a finger to his lips, Pedro warned, "Shhh…don't play anything too loud. This is a Federal Police station and we wouldn't want anyone to get the wrong idea."

Pedro knocked and a deep voice bid us to enter. Middle-aged, with thinning hair and a chest covered with medals and decorations, the chief rose and smiled, shaking our hands as Pedro introduced us. While Jill and I sat on an overstuffed couch, four or five other workers trickled in, quiet and curious. As Pedro handed me the guitar, I realized how long it had been since I'd played, especially in front of an audience. I was nervous. A love song I'd written for Jill was the softest one I knew. Everyone listened attentively as she and I sang in harmony, my fingers fumbling at the chords. As we finished, our audience clapped enthusiastically, calling in English for "More one! More one!" Still singing in a hushed voice, I played another, feeling more relaxed.

I could tell by the way Pedro's fingers were moving restlessly in his lap that he was itching to get the instrument in his hands. Concluding my second number, I passed him the guitar. Until that moment I would have described Pedro as mild mannered. But the instant that guitar touched his palms, he was transformed into a wild man.

"Jojo was a man who thought he was a woman, but he was another man! Get back! Get back! Get back to where you once belonged…." Pedro cut loose with throaty vocals and exaggerated facial gestures, rendering the classic Beatles tune with more emotion than the original. Next he sang a Brazilian song that set the whole office slapping their legs in rhythm. One woman swayed sensuously back and forth beneath her tight dress, dancing around the office.

"Shake-a-shake-shake-a-shake-a,…" the police chief had picked up a matchbox and was jiggling it back and forth like a rattle, his face one broad smile. Even in a Federal Police station it took only the slightest excuse to bring out the fun-loving side of Brazilians, who are always ready to celebrate for any reason or no reason.

Pedro played several more songs, all in Portuguese, the words and music blending together with a smoothness and fluidity that can't be matched in English.

"Well, it is time for us to go home," he said, fingernails strumming the last chord. The clock on the wall read five-thirty.

"Thank you for everything," I said.

"I wish you a good trip."

Everyone gathered to shake our hands before we left, except the police chief, who smiled and snapped to a salute. I saluted him right back and he laughed. Then Jill and I were out the door, Pedro waving as we walked out to the main road, where we caught a bus for Riacho Doce Beach and our green tent, *sem numero*.

★

Arthur Dawson is the author of A Passport from the Elements, *which chronicles a three-year journey he and his wife made around the world, traveling by sailboat, elephant, dugout canoe, steam train, and at least one bus with no brakes. Since their return home, he's been a little more stationary, teaching poetry to elementary school children and writing in a studio he built near Jack London's former ranch in Glen Ellen, California.*

PART THREE

GOING YOUR OWN WAY

✳

First Tango in Ladakh

Blindness can be a function of seeing.

SPRING CAME AND I FELT CLAUSTROPHOBIC, HEMMED IN BY THE city. Meanwhile, I had fallen in love with a whimsical and unpredictable ballerina. In fact, she was so unpredictable that by the end of June she had vanished in an ultimate pirouette. That was how I found myself embarking on a most extraordinary journey. Someone told me that she had gone to India, to the Himalayas, Kashmir, and Ladakh.

Ladakh. I tried to remember. Years ago I had seen some photographs of a fertile valley amid a fantastic wilderness of stone. The air was so thin that you could distinguish the texture of the rock, crevasses, and stratified folding, and beyond, towering above, the far snowcapped peaks of the mountains.

I had always been reticent about going to India. I felt that I needed to know more about it, that such a huge subcontinent should not be experienced haphazardly. Nevertheless, today I am off to India on an impulse.

Standing in the middle of New Delhi airport with my bag, I am suddenly aware of the folly of my venture. I do not know India; I have never been here before. And I am blind. How do I get to Kashmir, the Himalayas, when I do not even know how to get out of this airport or where to end the night? I left New York so suddenly that I had no time to call anyone for advice or practical information. It must be around one o'clock in the morning, but judging from the hubbub in this vast hall, you would think it was the middle of the day. Footsteps, hurried yet slack, pass me on all sides. I attempt to stop them, but in vain; they are driven by their karma to urgent business from which, I fully realize, I am excluded. I feel utterly helpless. I have been told that there is no plane to Srinagar before three o'clock tomorrow afternoon. I am exhausted from lack of sleep and badly need a shower.

"Sir!" A hand is tapping my arm. "Sir! Can we help you?" Before I have time to answer, my passport, bag, and a fistful of money are whisked away. I am left standing alone. Everything happens so fast that I have no time to ask the people who they are or, for that matter, to count my money. Hardly have I arrived in India, land of Gandhi, birthplace of nonviolence, than I am stripped of my belongings; yet, I admit, without violence.

More than half an hour has gone by. I am considering going back to New York when all of a sudden my passport is thrust into my hand with my money stuck between the pages, changed into rupees. Somebody grabs hold of my wrist and pulls me along at such a speed that I have difficulty following. This is an abduction!

We are now outside on the sidewalk in the hot, turbulent Indian night. A taxi is hailed, my bag put in the back, a hotel name given.

"Auto-rickshaw, three-wheel taxi, sir. Very cheap, only thirty rupees to your hotel. Good-bye. God bless you, sir." I am flabbergasted. "Wait! How can I thank you? You have been fantastic! Let me give you something." No answer. I extend my hand and meet only hot air. "Who were they?" The rickshaw driver laughs. "Beggars, sir, beggars."

The small vehicle zigzags to avoid the potholes. Cramped between the roof and my bag, I endure endless bumps and vibrations. Like everyone else, my driver ensures our safety by honking all the way.

The Imperial Hotel is an old-fashioned building on Janpath with vast rooms. At six a.m., after a short but restful night, I start looking for the swimming pool. A very old man in a very clean loincloth and turban, with measured movements and a vaporous voice, leads me from the changing room to the pool.

My vision, which is just as real as yours, just as unique, enables me to describe here the whiteness of a turban, the shades of brown in the rock, and the expression of greed on a face. Believe me when I tell you that this visionary state overcomes me unawares. It is almost as if the generosity of the world surrenders itself to me if I wish. The swimming pool is deserted. I dive in. The water is still cold from the night before. I swim enthusiastically, tearing twenty hours of flight from my muscles. Suddenly, something hits my forehead. For a fraction of a second, I think I am going to smash into the wall. I extend my hand and find no obstacle. I start swimming again, gently at first, but as I regain self-confidence, throwing myself into it once more, I am again forced to stop. A hard object actually brushes against me. This time I am faster, and in one fell swoop, as if catching a fly, I grab hold of…my cane! Yes, my cane, just as the old man's voice directs my attention from the edge of the pool, "This way, sir, this way!"

He had noticed how I guide myself by following my cane. Since it was obvious that I could not use it to swim with, he was running around the pool, pointing it in front of my nose to indicate the line I should follow. Rescued by beggars, led while swimming by a galloping old man—I am enchanted by such irrationality. I may not run into any serious difficulty in India after all.

That afternoon, the plane is postponed every hour, and I end up sleeping at the airport. Finally, we take off on time…the following day.

In the warm Srinagar afternoon, I jolt along in an old taxi sent by one of the houseboats on Dal Lake. At the lake we abandon the car for a kind of gondola called a *shikara*. Showing me to a wide seat covered with cushions, the driver tells me to stretch out and relax like a rajah.

The mountains on the north horizon, the lake, all are still. Only the birds move over the evening waters. The sound of hawks cawing is somehow sinister. It must be past five o'clock. The children are coming home from school. So much laughter. The boatman's hook hits the hull at regular intervals with a thud. Without seeing, I perceive all this beauty—the mountains, the lake, the floating islands, the sunset blurring softly—and it stabs me like a dagger. I plunge my hand into the water. It is warm, thick. Half a million human beings defecate into it daily.

The houseboat is built entirely of sandalwood and smells like a pencil sharpener. All around, the creaking of floorboards. It must come from the many gangways linking the houses to each other. A cup of tea is brought in silently. A gin and tonic would be more appropriate. Life seems to flow here, more than anywhere else, in a sort of static frenzy or frantic stillness. A breeze coming down from the glaciers makes the lake shiver. How am I going to find her?

In the pale morning, I board a *shikara* padded with stuffed rags and shaded from the sun by a plastic patchwork. We set off for the palace of the maharajah of Kashmir, which has now become the Oberoi Palace Hotel. Built around 1925, it stands in the middle of lawns like a great white elephant overlooking the lake.

Doormen welcome me with pomp and circumstance. At the reception, I am told that the young lady has indeed been staying here but left two days ago.

I decide to review the situation over a cup of tea served on the lawn. An acrid smell rising from the lake, carried over on the gentle breeze, mingles with the scent of Darjeeling tea and marmalade.

"Good morning, sir. Allow me to introduce myself. Here is my card." He reads, slowly, over my shoulder, "Kemala, that is my name, sir. Guide No. 1 for hunting. Underneath it is written, Srinagar, Kashmir, India. Please keep it, sir. You are looking for one lady. I know where she is."

I ask him to sit down. His voice sounds virile and wily. An old fox, in fact, he smells of earth, leaves, and rain. He must be around fifty years old. "This lady has gone to see a holy man. He is my friend. I can take you there."

I have no illusions whatsoever. The old fox may well have invented the whole story, but it does not matter. He says that there is no road to the village and that it is two days' ride from Sonamarg. A car will take us to meet the horses. I suggest we leave tomorrow. We agree on a price, and, busy already, he stands up, touches me on the forehead, and walks away across the lawn.

Next day we drive for three hours. At the edge of a saffron field that has a sickly sweet smell, a boy is waiting for us with three ponies, one of which is laden with a tent, supplies, and kitchen utensils.

For several hours we ride up rocky paths that become progressively steeper. By evening we have reached a grassy plateau dotted with trees and shriveled bushes at the edge of a glacier. The sun has slipped behind the ridge, and the cold from this mass of ice at proximity penetrates our clothes. The boy, who has been trotting all the way alongside his horse, gathers some dead wood and builds a small fire. The water is soon singing in the kettle. Behind us, the fettered horses munch the hard, dry grass. My thigh muscles are stiff from the ride. Suddenly we are very far away, and instinctively we huddle together around the little fire. Kemala drinks his tea with long, noisy slurps. We eat a meal of rice and curry cooked over the embers. Kemala reminisces about hunting and women. He muddles up the furry animals with the pretty ladies. Wood fires, nights on high plateaus, incite fantasizing. Kemala guarantees that it will not rain tonight.

All is quiet. The silence is awesome. Lying in the grass, in this wide open space under the stars, cradled in the warmth of my sleeping bag, I drift off into the wisdom of uncertainty.

We leave before dawn and soon reach the other side of the plateau, now covered with a cedar forest. Birdsong echoes through the undergrowth. Followed by the boy, Kemala takes a shortcut too steep for me to attempt. I let go the reins and let the little horse follow the trail. The other two ponies are waiting for me ahead. We ride on for a while, until they leave me again for another shortcut. Once more their steps grow fainter. Then there is silence. I sink into a formidable mineral and botanical world. Sometimes the way is barred by a small torrent, which my pony crosses, meticulously putting down his feet, punctuating the difficult moments with an unforeseen movement of his withers to get us over the obstacle. Suddenly, a rumbling resonates up above, rolling down into the valley. And again—thunder!

All at once I realize that I must have been riding alone for more than half an hour. Where have the others gone? I bring the horse to a halt. A few raindrops fall on my face. Taking hold of the reins again, I urge the little horse forward. Having listened to me, he too is worried now. After a while, soaked through and freezing, I jump down by a tree trunk as big as a medieval tower and flatten myself against the bark while the horse leans against me. I am buried in this forest, these mountains, this India. There is no question about it, I am well and truly lost.

Suddenly Kemala emerges from the rain like a sad, vegetal Don Quixote. He dismounts agilely and comes and leans against my shoulder. His voice cracks like dry wood. He says that the rain has put the horses off the scent. He hands me a lighted cigarette. "Only small rain. Rainy season is finished." Without another word, we wait in silence.

A few hours later, under a clear sky, we reach our destination. A small, unruly, and boisterous crowd is standing outside the holy man's house. We walk through the groups of people, who step aside to let us through. An old woman greets us, laughing. Kemala thrusts a plastic bag into my hand. "Fruit, sir, no money." But the woman has already snatched the bag away from me and is leading us to a room at the back of the house.

The room is dark, windowless. The noisy crowd outside has suddenly ceased to exist. I can hear the woman placing the bag of fruit before the man; then he speaks. His voice is gentle but firm. Didn't Kemala say he was a hundred and thirty years old? I would have said he was a hundred years younger. Kemala launches into a long-winded monologue, interrupted by the short, precise questions of the saint, then turns to me with disapproval in his voice. "He can do nothing for your eyes."

"Tell him I know, not to worry. Ask him about the young lady."

The holy man laughs. He asks that I sit on the mat near him. The tips of our knees are touching. He has placed one of my hands, the right one, on his knee. Under the cotton, his skin feels surprisingly young and elastic. And yet, if one is to believe Kemala, he lives here on this mat without having slept or eaten for years. He seems to be enjoying our meeting. I am conscious of this by the smile in his voice, the way he puts his hand on mine, flat on his knee. He says, "Learn to live slowly—that way there will be no hazard in death." Kemala translates.

As I leave him, I almost feel as though I am abandoning him to his strange destiny, sitting there on his cushion in this dark room with a crowd at his door. Perhaps he has felt my compassion, for he grabs hold of my hand again just as I am getting up and says, "Surviving life is everything." Kemala translates. I find the idea hilarious, and we laugh heartily together.

Back in Srinagar, the receptionist at the Oberoi says that the young lady most likely went on to Leh, the capital of Ladakh.

In the early dim gray morning, I board the plane for Leh. We fly over the rock face of the Himalayas, the col, and then a fluffy mass of cloud suspended between the mountains like an eiderdown beneath which lies the valley of Ladakh. After a while I realize that we are going around in circles. The man on my right, who has introduced himself as Krishna, a dry-fruit merchant, says that the pilot cannot find the hole in the cloud.

Suddenly the plane drops, leaving our stomachs in our mouths. The pilot found the hole. A few minutes later, we land.

A bit shattered, I disembark on the concrete runway amid the general excitement of guttural shouting and laughter. Beyond the runway, yet uncannily close, however, looms a formidable presence that reduces our little troop to a handful of ants. Krishna asks me where I am staying and recommends the Sankar Guest House.

As the taxi drives through the plain, Krishna does not say a word; he seems just as much in awe as I. We drive to Leh, through its main street swarming with animals and human beings.

The Sankar Guest House is a small squat building that stands on a hillock at the north end of town. Already the land here begins its ascent toward the surrounding monstrosity; its mass does not seem to grow out of the earth but to descend from the sky.

"Jullay…Jullay…" is the local greeting. Smiling voices, quiet and mischievous. My room is like a bare cell. There is absolutely nothing to disturb the mind. Outside my window, conversations linger on in the pure air. Immense, the void in the valley reverberates against all the rock, assailing us. The ephemeral tender green cultivation enhances the hardness of the rock. Naked children are jumping off a bridge into the icy water. Their cries pierce the air like raining pins. A sudden breeze enters the summer of my room. I strain to listen to the void outside. Suddenly I am filled with an intense desire, a mad, aimless desire to go out on the plain and climb up to the horizon. I start to laugh. A laughter provoked by the absurdity of my situation and by the altitude, which has gone to my head. The valley of Ladakh is situated thirteen thousand feet above sea level.

Next morning, Krishna and I walk to the little bank of Leh to change some money. The clerk recognizes me immediately as the "strange tourist" whose arrival was announced on the local radio.

In the street I can feel Krishna's plump body shaking with laughter. I listen to footsteps—small steps, dragging steps, bright skipping steps—thudding on the ground. "Listen," I say to Krishna. "Stop laughing. The girl I'm looking for is here. Help me find her." But how is he going to recognize her? I assure him that as soon as she sees me, she will stop dead in her tracks and stare at me in such a way that he will not be able to miss her.

Despite all the rupees that we lavish on the rapacious Kashmiris, the hotels yield no result. Krishna suggests the Dreamland Restaurant, where all the Westerners hang out. To get there we struggle through the market, an extraordinary mixture of smells, noises, and mud.

As we walk through the door, Krishna squeezes my arm: "There she is!" Heart pounding, I step forward, when he suddenly pulls me back. "Now there are three women staring at you!" He laughs. "You are a strange tourist, my friend."

In silence, we walk back up the road in the cool evening air. On the way we pass a peasant pushing his donkey along by kicking his behind, while his friend, laughing, is doing the same to him.

"Since you can't find your girl, why don't you come to Rizong with me to buy apricots from the Julichen nuns?" I agree.

Next day, in glorious light, the jeep speeds along the wide, muddy bank of the Indus. The river winds its way toward the Lamayuru pass, flowing by the ancient monastery of Alchi, then dips from the Himalayan heights into the Arabian Sea, bringing wealth and death, alluvial fertility and floods.

Suddenly Krishna starts cursing. "The road has been cut off! There has been a landslide." On our right a gentle breeze whistles through the tall trees; on our left a vigorous torrent gushes where the road has been destroyed. We hide the car in the bushes. We cross the fault and continue on foot. My bag is not meant for trekking. I keep shifting it from shoulder to shoulder, but after a while both shoulders hurt just as much. I try to relieve the pain by carrying it on my head, but the load only makes my foot stiff, forcing me to walk like a robot.

We fork left and cross the torrent through a shallow ford. The ice-cold water soothes my aching feet. The sun is now directly over us; it must be midday. Sitting on round boulders at the edge of the little river, we make a meal out of chapatis and cold chicken.

We resume our rugged walk along a steep path. I desperately keep shifting my bag, trying hard to avoid the question burning my lips: how much farther? We keep on climbing in undisturbed silence except for the cries of a few birds of prey. At last we hear voices. We have arrived at Rizong and the apricot orchards of the Julichen nuns.

It is a humble retreat. We pass under the arch that leads through the main building to an open courtyard that smells of apricots. The nuns greet us with much hilarity and gentle hissing, owing to their toothless mouths. They are all old, ageless, drier than their apricots drying in the sun. They invite us to drink rancid butter diluted in tea and offer us apricots. Afraid of catching dysentery, I stuff them into my pocket. The nuns chatter incessantly and regularly throw me a "Jullay!" I feel them to be extremely light, as light as the air around us. They are stoning the apricots before drying them on the terrace overlooking a tiny valley. Krishna describes them to

me. They are dressed in rags, never bothering to mend or sew their
torn skirts, bodices, or shawls. He says that he is going to do business with them but that it will take time; therefore, we will have
to spend the night here.

In the evening, which goes on forever, two nuns who seem
even older than the rest bring us an indefinable, frugal supper. We
eat it in front of the stone hut that serves as the convent guest
house. Rather than spend the night in that windowless hovel, I decide to find a relatively flat piece of ground where I can put down
a mat. The only possible place, after getting rid of the stones, is the
path that leads to the Rizong monastery. Despite Krishna's disapproval, something to do with the effect of the moon on the "already lunatic spirits," I spend a delightful night in my sleeping bag
on the roof of the world. Between the infinite and myself, I can
hear an imperceptible whistling—God whistling between his teeth,
between the high, sharp ice peaks, in the night.

In an infernal racket, all the mountain demons tumble down on
me at once. Sounds of iron banging on rock, gongs resounding,
shrieks of laughter. Dust is getting into my nostrils, throat, and
ears. I sit up with a bolt. "What the...?"

"Jullay...Jullay..." answer voices. They are not demons but a
group of monks who have started at dawn to repair the track gul-
lied by the rains. I roll up my sleeping bag and mat, then, helped by
a young monk, go and wake up Krishna. In his stone box, he has
not heard a thing and laughs when he sees me covered with dust.

As I wash in the little spring near the hostel, Krishna informs
me that he had bought the nuns' harvest and is ready to go
down. I point out that although he has found what he wanted, I
still have not.

I do not go down to the plain with Krishna. I am beginning to
enjoy this adventure. From beggars to a galloping old man, from
Kemala to Krishna, I realize that if I am willing to be patient,
something will always happen, somebody will appear, and even
though I may get stuck, it will never be for long. The prodigious
energy of this land and its people will push me onward as far and
as long as I want.

At midday I accompany the road-worker monks back up to their monastery. The same young monk who helped me wake up Krishna takes a firm grip on my hand and, laughing all the while, asks me questions in Ladakhi that I do not understand. We have been walking for some time, and the path is very steep. My bag seems heavier than ever.

Suddenly, the characteristic hammering of little hooves on the ground. A mountain dweller and his donkey. Amid many Jullays, I try to explain that I want to rent the donkey. Everyone laughs, but no one understands. Finally the man begins to suspect a change in the course of his journey when I take hold of the donkey's halter, forcing the animal to take a demi-volte, placing its tail where its head had been a few seconds before. Next, I poise my bag on its withers, sit astride the tiny mount, and, pointing up ahead, cry "Gompa!"—which means "monastery"—as you would cry "Charge!" There is a moment's silence, then everybody bursts out laughing. The owner agrees to twenty rupees, but the donkey has not been consulted. With all the obstinacy of its breed, it refuses to budge an inch. The young monk tries to push the animal, then remembers a universal technique and grabs hold of its tail, twisting it violently. Suddenly it takes off with a bolt, to its own surprise.

Finally the ground levels out. We enter a little circus-shaped valley. "Gompa," says one of the monks, taking my hand and pointing it up. Between the peaks the great monastery of Rizong stands in all its majesty.

As we reach the top of the steps, the monks g a t h e r around me. Among them I notice the voices of very young boys, children, little novices, no doubt. They laugh and

monastery in Ladakh

blurt out high-pitched interjections. Yet despite their constant energy, a sense of peace emanates from their brouhaha. They guide me to a terrace where I am presented to the rimpoche, the abbot of Rizong. He takes the fingers of my left hand; although I understand not a word of what he is saying, my fingers perceive that I am welcome. Beside him, a monk translates into somewhat tantric English. The rimpoche says: "Come under our roof and stay as long as you wish. The food is very bad. The people who come here from the West are usually sightseeing with their cameras. Not you. Why did you come to Ladakh?"

After a few days, the monks seem to have totally adopted me in a particular way and let me sleep on a high terrace: Lama Lampu, the translator, calls it the Terrace of Solitude.

In the morning, I hear sandals shuffling. "Jullay! Jullay!" It is Lama Lampu. He sits down. The cry of a bird of prey tears through the air, and way down in the valley, lost among the trees, I can hear water flowing. Lama Lampu touches my chest and laughs. He says that my insisting on sleeping in the open air leaves me vulnerable to all kinds of spirits who willingly enter into me. He says that my face is still dark from the night. We get up and go to breakfast on some miserable concoction.

Buzzing with activity, the kitchen is a square room with a high ceiling. In the middle a charcoal fire is kept burning all day long. The room is full of smoke; the vault, wall, shelves, all seem cooked; everything is black with soot except for the shiny brass and copper utensils. The smoke floats in the room without seeming to bother the monks, who melt into the monochrome background. Framed by the small openings pierced in the thick wall, the landscape seems all the brighter. We sit down by a window with our small wooden bowls.

Lama Lampu guides me everywhere, makes me touch everything, see everything. The great façade, with its classical, uncluttered, serene layout, hides an extraordinary labyrinth of corridors, passages, split levels, corners, and terraces jutting out under the sky. The original chaos, disorder of the soul, ferreting through thought. Unexpected passages, windows looking out onto walls, rooms apparently without purpose. But after a while, one realizes that all this imbroglio of architecture corresponds to well-determined functions, that there is reason in the madness. In the main sanctuary he stands on my left, his right arm around my waist, and takes my right hand, not only to direct me but to apply it to books centuries old, to the chair reserved for the Dalai Lama, to the multiple statues of the incarnations of Buddha. He spares me nothing. And, of course, according to the rules, we walk around the sanctuary clockwise. A sequence from the film *Some Like It Hot* springs to my mind and I close my hand over Lama Lampu's and draw him into a tango, keeping the beat with onomatopoeia. "Ta-DUM, ta-DUM, tadada-DUM…" There is no question that this is the first time a tango has ever been danced in a Himalayan monastery. The monks guffaw, and my behavior, which surprises even me, does not seem to shock them at all.

*

Before being blinded by muggers in New York City, Hugues de Montalembert was a painter, filmmaker, and writer. In his book, Eclipse, *which was translated from the French into four languages, he writes about his blinding and search for a cure. He still travels widely and writes regularly for French and U.S. publications. He lives in Paris.*

* ✴ *

Murderer's Eggs

Strange creatures can be found in the
central desert of Baja California.

AFTER LEAVING THE PAVED ROAD I HAD SOME TROUBLE LOCATING
the arroyo. It was dusk, and the features of the land were all beginning to look the same. I made rapid drives up two or three
openings in the terrain only to encounter rock walls. Finally, in the
last of the light, I recognized a distinctive portion of the skyline of
jagged hills up ahead that could lead us through the arroyo and
into a valley. Across that valley, another arroyo leads past the remains of a deserted old *rancho*, then into a canyon where lay the
long abandoned Mission San Borja, Lucretia Borgia's legacy to the
New World.

I was traveling with Garrett Culhane and Matt Tully, two friends
from school. Matthew is five foot eight, with a beautiful physique
and a perfectly silly-looking tattoo of a cherub and a crescent
moon on his right shoulder. His shoulder-length hair and trim
beard are both flame red. His hair is so thick and curly it looks like
a 17th-century cavalier's wig. If he traded his gold-rimmed glasses
for a rapier and a dueling pistol the picture would be complete.
He's a fun guy, but he tends to forget that there is a tomorrow.

Garrett grew up on a ranch in the California Central Valley,
but he looks like he stepped out of an E.M. Forster novel about

turn of the century England. He is tall, lean and angular with black hair and neat mustache. His jaw juts forward handsomely. His favorite cloth is tweed. He is cerebral and reflective and tends to preface his questions with "Well now, Richard, let me ask you something." He likes to have philosophical conversations that often become so convoluted he gets lost in them. He is also a first-rate mechanic.

Garrett and Matt were behind me in Garrett's rebuilt 1959 Willys jeep, panelled version. I led the way in my four-wheel-drive vehicle, the Argo. The normally clear skies were full of January clouds and a mist had risen from the ground. The sun had fully set and the darkness was so dense and so thick it was palpable. It gobbled up my headlight beams in mere yards. The recent annual rains had turned the dry water courses into gooey bogs and we would have to cross them in the dark. We crept along in low four-wheel drive, keeping in close radio contact.

We had been rolling for over an hour when Matt radioed, "Argo, be advised we are overheating."

"Cause?"

"Unknown. Will keep you advised."

Within minutes he called again to say, "Argo, Argo! We've got to stop, we've got to stop, we're red-lining!"

"Ten-four," I answered. "I'm coming to help." I judged from the lights in my rear-view mirror that they were about forty or fifty feet behind me, so I cut the engine and hopped out and began walking toward the Willys. The mist was not uniform like a fog; it was a crazy mist, hanging in clumps and swirls with currents of clear air between them. It puffed up from the water courses and slid down hillsides and curled itself around the cacti and cirrio and other solid objects. It made the Willys seem much closer than it really was. I turned around and could no longer see the white form of the Argo.

When I reached the other vehicle the guys had the hood up, and in the reflected light of the headlamps I could see a stream of hot water drizzling down to the ground and making a big, steamy puddle. "Have you isolated the leak yet?" I asked.

"No," Garrett said. "It's almost dry now. We'll have to fill it up and try again. Let me ask you something, do you have plenty of water?"

"Five gallons. But from the look of that stream it won't get us back to the highway."

We filled the radiator and turned on the engine. Water gushed from a broken seam in the radiator's exit port. The damage could hardly have been worse. If it were a broken hose we might have fixed it, as we carried a few spares; but this situation required removing the radiator and then having it repaired by a welder. The nearest welder was in Guerrero Negro. I would need a full day to get there, a day to have the radiator repaired, and a day to get back. I would have to take Matt with me in case I should have some breakdown, or injury, end up in jail, or who knows what. Garrett would have to keep his own philosophical company in the desert for the next three days. Happy New Year.

Somewhere in the mist a dog barked. "Was that a dog?" Matt asked.

"Must be a coyote," I said. "Got to be a coyote. No dogs out here." The dog barked again. In the headlamp beams a puff of drifting mist began to darken and take form. As it came near it assumed the shape of a man with rifle. A dog shape trotted alongside. When he was still a silhouette he stopped and hefted the rifle in the crook of his arm.

"*¿Quien es?*" he hollered. Who's there?

"*Amigos,*" I answered. "*Hombres que necesitan ayuda. ¿Quien es usted señor?*" Friends. Men who need help. Who are you, sir?

The shape paused. He said something to his dog, who then sat down and licked his chops. He came forward and with each step divested himself of mist. He came to within arm's length and stopped. He was a short, dark man, strongly built, with a curly beard. He was scruffy and dirty and lost-looking, and he eyed us with curiosity and delight, especially Matt's bountiful cascades of firehair. He thrust a stubby hand out to anyone who would take it and said, "*Manuel, me llamo Manuel. A su servicio, señores.*" I am Manuel, at your service, sirs.

He spoke no English, so I translated introductions. He told us he was living in the ancient *rancho* a few miles from the mission. He lived alone.

"Why are you carrying the rifle?" I asked him.

"Because I thought you might be cattle rustlers. I have a few head and I thought you might be after them."

"Cattle rustlers, out here?" I asked.

"Who else would come here?" he shrugged. "Tell me, sirs. Why, in fact, are you here?"

We told him of our quest to San Borja, and then we told him of our trouble. He looked very excited and said, "Oh let me, let me." He took my flashlight and crawled under the hood, half his body disappearing between the V-8 engine and the radiator. He fingered the breach, then came up smiling. I told him it needed "*soldadura*," welding. "Maybe not," he said, gesturing up the road. "At my *ranchito* I have a paste, an epoxy, that I mix together and use to repair metals. Maybe it can work to fix your radiator."

I translated this to the others. Garrett looked hopefully at Manuel and said, "Right now?"

"*¿Ahora mismo?*" I asked Manuel.

"Please, gentlemen, it's dark. It's no time to work, or to drive in the desert." Eagerly he said, "But I would be delighted if you would be my guests tonight. I can fix you some dinner. I can give you fresh eggs; I have chickens. You like coffee?"

"Hey, I'm for it," Matt said. "I'm starving." Matt is never not starving.

"How far is it?" Garrett asked. "Will we have to leave the Willys behind?"

The *rancho* was only about fifty yards ahead of the Argo. Manuel ran ahead. When we rolled up a few minutes later he was rousting his chickens for all the eggs he could find. "Come in, come in," he said with a sweeping gesture and a grin, as we walked into his kitchen. "Sit down. Be comfortable." His little house consisted of this room and a bedroom. It was lit by a kerosene lamp and candles, and at the sink he drew water with a hand pump. All was dirt and dishevelment, but putting a hand on his heart and a pious look on his face he said, "I have very little, but what I have I give with all my heart." Matt pulled a bottle of wine out of his jacket; Manuel glowed.

Manuel had collected six fresh, brown eggs, very large, and set about preparing them on his kerosene stove. "I have no tortillas, I hope you won't mind. I'll make you something similar to *huevos rancheros*. It's my own dish." He made a soupy *ranchero* sauce of onions, chili peppers, garlic, and tomato sautéed in *manteca*. To that he added cooked macaroni. He broke three eggs into the pan of sauce. The others he broke into another pan and fried them, again using *manteca*. The eggs in the sauce were poached semi hard; those fried were sunny side up and the yolks ran when cut. He served us each a fried egg and a poached egg, both covered with the macaroni salsa.

I pushed some of my macaroni over onto the fried egg. I cut the egg up and swirled it, letting the fat, yellow yolk coat the pasta. The pasta was still hot enough to cook the yolk into a tasty glaze. On the other side of my plate I cut up the poached egg and mashed the yolk into the piquant sauce, making it thicker and more savory. The *manteca* gave the whole dish a rich smoothness and produced a warm and satisfying full feeling in the belly. Matt poured the rosy red wine and we feasted. Manuel beamed and politely tried not to guzzle the Cabernet Sauvignon.

After dinner we decided that whiskey was called for and Garrett brought forth a bottle. Manuel was agog at his good luck. He had been living out there for months, he said, "with no comforts." Garrett poured healthy draughts all around and Manuel asked us to tell him our story. We described our lives to him, told him of work, of school, travel, war and peace. He followed each story with interest, he savored every detail. He had been starving for human company and this was nourishment for him.

He became effusive with good cheer. "My friends," he said, suddenly inspired, "we have a custom where I come from. When men are friends, and they enjoy each other's stories and food and drink, they exchange *mustachios*." So saying he reached up to the corner of his mustache and, grabbing on to several whiskers, gave a snappy tug and yanked them out! Grinning, he held them forth between thumb and forefinger, the white roots like little flower bulbs at the ends of black stalks. "For you," he said. Not knowing what else to do we each took one, muttering a confused "*gracias*."

Manuel sat there grinning, looking at us each in turn, waiting for a response. With a shrug, Matt reached up to his mustache and ripped out a shard of hairs that made a sound like grass being pulled from the ground. "There you go, Manuel," he said, "and one for all of you, too," and he passed them around.

Garrett seemed to think the whole thing hilarious and said, "Ha ha. And here's some for you," as he reached for both ends of his mustache and tore out his offering, sharing them with all. Manuel collected his mementoes and promised to keep them in a special place. I was so glad that I was the only clean-shaven member of this bizarre ritual of male bonding and said, "Damn! I wish I had a mustache!"

Lest this go any further and we start driving nails into our arms or slicing off bits of our flesh, I asked Manuel to tell us his story. He sat back for a moment and took a breath, as though gathering his powers. He requested a refill. Taking a sip, and rolling it on his tongue pensively, he began: "I'm here, my friends, for gold." We leaned closer. Taking another sip and gauging our interest he said, "I know gold. I know how to find it. It's here, my friends, in these hills. The Spaniards, they were no good at finding gold. They built the missions and found souls to save but they weren't good at finding gold. That's why it's still here," he whispered, "and I'm going to find it." He looked at his empty glass. Hands rushed to fill it.

He drew a lump of ore from his pocket and set it on the table. For a moment the only sound was breathing. "Look," he urged. "Look. If you know gold, you can see I'm going to be rich." We all leaned toward the quartzy piece of rock and peered into its interstices, as though it were a crystal ball, looking for a golden future.

"Let me have a closer look," I said. "When I was seventeen I worked in a gold mine." I picked it up and, turning it over said, "Mmm."

"Does it look like good stuff?" Matt asked as Manuel sat proudly looking on.

"Mmm."

"Well, what do you think? You think it's the real thing?" Garrett asked.

"Mmm."

"Good eh?" said Manuel.

"Uh...mmm...er...I can't tell. It's been a long time since I worked in the gold mine, and that was just during summer vacation."

Manuel took the ore and said, "I'll show you." He got up, a little woozily. Having been so long without "comforts" he was getting "comfortable" pretty fast. He dug through a wooden box and came up with a battered pair of binoculars. Looking through the big end he focused on the ore with the small end and said, "Here, look." We all looked. We saw nothing, but said nothing. We just nodded, not letting on that we didn't "know gold," and wondering how you could know it by looking through the wrong end of a pair of binoculars. Manuel helped himself to more whiskey.

The liquor coursed through him, and he waxed expansive as he described all the things he was going to do when he was rich, all the places he would go, all the women he would have; they would all be blondes. Then he suddenly changed the subject. "You see that saddle over there," he said, pointing to a ruined-looking pile of old leather. "Pancho Villa rode in that saddle. It belonged to him. You know Pancho Villa, the great general?"

"Oh yes," we all nodded. "Pancho Villa, the great general."

"He was from Sonora," Manuel told us. "I'm from Sonora, too." Lurching across the room he picked up his old rifle. I noticed that the butt was cracked and held together with electrical tape. He brandished it at us and said, "And this rifle was used in the Mexican revolution. It killed many men. Many men."

Matt looked like he was going to hide the whiskey, but I grabbed it and poured Manuel the stiffest drink his glass could hold. "*Salúd*," I said. "Let's drink to Pancho Villa, the great general!" Patriotically Manuel drank the health of the general, draining his glass. I refilled it.

"My friends," said Manuel, "I told you I'm from Sonora. You know why I'm now in Baja California?"

"For gold," we all said.

"Well, yes. But you know why I'm also in Baja California?" Cradling his rifle he sat down and eyed us all dizzily. Absentmindedly he reached into a pocket and pulled out a handful of bullets.

"Let's drink to Sonora!" Matt said. Manuel, rifle in one hand and bullets in the other, considered his glass. He put the bullets back in his pocket and drank to Sonora. I refilled his glass.

Manuel continued, "I'm here because I killed a man in Sonora. He was an Indian. I caught him cheating me at cards. I didn't have my famous rifle with me," he said, patting it on the breach. "So I killed him with my knife. He was a big man, but I'm fast, and my knife was big. I don't have the knife anymore because I left it in the Indian. Damned Indian," he muttered.

His rifle was getting heavy so he leaned it against a wall and turned his attentions to his glass which I kept full. "Yes, I had to run from Sonora. The police wouldn't get me because they're my friends. I had to run from the Indians! So I went to Sinaloa. And what do you think? I killed another Indian, over a woman! This time the police wanted to get me, so I ran away to Baja." His head drooping low, his face inches from the table, he murmured his last words of the evening: "And now I'm going to get rich and find gold."

He sank into a little heap of whiskey-soaked flesh. We laid him in his lumpy bed and covered him with his filthy blankets. We looked at each other and sniggered. Pancho Villa's saddle, a revolutionary rifle, two dead Indians, and a lost gold mine all in one night; we'd never heard whiskey talk so much.

The next morning Manuel was up and about, hung over and still drunk at the same time. After giving us his epoxy he kept getting in the way of things, so we dispatched him quickly and painlessly with a few more drinks. After making our repairs we set a big lockback knife, as a present, on his table and left him sleeping. About a week later, in Bahía de Los Angeles, we met Don

Guillermo, who turned out to be *el Dueño*, the owner of the land
Manuel occupies. "Was he kind to you?" Don Guillermo asked.

"Oh yes. He gave us dinner. And we gave him whiskey," and
we all chuckled.

"You gave him whiskey?" Don Guillermo asked with visible
concern.

"Uh…yeah. After all, he was very hospitable to us."

"*Señores*. You should be very careful who you drink with
around here. Manuel can be violent when he's drunk. He's already
killed two men, that we know of."

So, okay, Manuel is, indeed, a murderer. He has conducted two
of his fellows out of this world untimely to the next. *Que vayan con
Dios and Amen*. But when he follows them he will, at least, have left
behind his single, humble contribution to the happiness of the living. His little culinary offering stays active in my recipe file, where
it frequently satisfies the appetites of my friends and garners me
much praise. It was no less a personage than Brillat-Savarin, the
great 18th-century gastronome who said, "The discovery of a new
dish does more for human happiness than the discovery of a star."
Even if the telescope is wielded by a man with the curse of Cain,
the discovery is a worthy one:

Murderer's Eggs

½ Spanish onion, diced
1 not-so-hot green chili pod, seeded and diced
garlic to taste, minced
6 oz. can tomato sauce
½ cup cooked (*al dente*) elbow macaroni or rigatoni
2 eggs
1 tablespoon cilantro, chopped
salt and pepper
manteca (You can use butter or olive oil and the result may
    be healthier but it won't be as satisfying.)

Sauté the vegetables in the *manteca* over medium heat till soft. Add tomato sauce, salt, and pepper. A dash of Worcester is good, too. Cook five minutes over low heat. Stir in pasta and cilantro. Push the pasta outward from the center, making a space for the eggs. Break the eggs into the pan and cover them with sauce, being careful not to rupture the yolks. Cover the pan, reduce heat to very low, and let the eggs poach three minutes or to desired doneness.

★

Richard Sterling is a writer, editor, lecturer, and insatiable traveler. Earlier in life he served in the Navy and was a Silicon Valley engineer, but stability and respectability lost out over wanderlust. Since taking up the pen he has been honored by the James Beard Foundation for his food writing, and by the Lowell Thomas Awards for his travel literature. He is the editor of Food: A Taste of the Road *and* The Adventure of Food, *and the author of several books in the Lonely Planet World Food series, as well as* The Fearless Diner *and* The Fire Never Dies, *from which this story was excerpted. He is based in Berkeley, California, where he is often politically incorrect.*

MICHELE ANNA JORDAN

. * .

Circle of Gold

*Two birds take flight one fine
evening in San Francisco.*

IT WAS A MAY MORNING, A LONG TIME AGO IN SONOMA COUNTY
when the population was a small fraction of what it is now. I awoke
very early, easy to do in Lakeville with my bedroom window facing the low hills east of Petaluma. As I made my morning tea I
could see the nearly full moon dropping into the horizon behind
the long row of eucalyptus trees that always reminded me, I told
Gina and Nicolle, toddlers then, of a broccoli parade. There was
some pretty goldenrod print fabric on my nightstand, with some
black cotton lace and a soft piece of black velvet, which by noon I
had transformed into a skirt, long and flowing, and a blouse with
lace trim and velvet yoke. I drove the fifteen or so miles to the university, where I found my friend Estelle waiting for me, dressed
from head to toe in black and yellow, one of the many coincidences
we later considered with great seriousness. With her head of thick,
wild auburn curls, my long reddish-blond locks and our color-
coordinated outfits, we looked like a pair of exotic birds.

Anapendulum—now known as the Commons but then in-
triguingly named as the companion of The Pit, the bohemian
campus coffeehouse that is now part of the expanded Sonoma
State University bookstore—was full to overflowing that Saturday,

as a vibrant crowd of fans awaited Anaïs Nin. She dazzled us all when she appeared in her fine chiseled beauty, draped in a floor-length black cape, her signature braids crowning her head. She seemed to float on the wave of our expectations and, though I remember nothing of the content of her talk, I have a profound physical memory of its emotional impact. Her words cast a magic spell over us all, and I remember that I cried when I shook her hand, so long and delicate and frail: birdlike, as she was then.

My yellow Volkswagen had broken down on the way to campus, but the glory of the day was such that I had simply gotten out and hitched a ride from the next car to come along, refusing to speculate that car trouble might put an end to the adventure Estelle and I had planned. When I informed her of the mechanical misfortune, she offered a typically spirited response. "Let's go to San Francisco anyway," she said, and we hitchhiked back to my car to get my coat, actually a long black knit shawl, my warmest garment in those days. At the car, I decided to give it a try and when it started on the first attempt, we considered it a sign and headed off towards the Golden Gate to claim San Francisco as our own.

We walked around Union Square and as the sun began to set, decided to have dinner. The place we tried first, a new French cafe, turned us away because they had run out of food. We tried four or five different restaurants and were either turned away or, in one case, left after being seated because our waiter was a jerk. As we left the final restaurant, a cable car was passing by, no waiting behind the line, just dangerous, mid-street boarding and friendly, spirited conductors. We asked for a recommendation and the conductor said, "Just wait, I'll tell you when to get off." As the cable car groaned into its turn onto Jackson Street, he said, "Get off now, eat there," pointing to The Coachman's Bar with The Oak Tree restaurant inside.

The bar itself was a tiny, cozy place and at the entrance to the dining room we were greeted by a friendly, proper host with a charming British accent. He handed us each a carnation and seated us near the window, where every few minutes another cable car rattled by. A quick view of the menu revealed that we had ventured into a world quite unlike our own, where student budgets and the casual counterculture of Sonoma in the mid-'70s defined our diet. At that point, I don't believe I had ever ordered a glass of wine and we were suddenly confronted with choices and prices that were staggeringly out of our league. But it was a special night, we said, as we ordered mixed grill and a bottle of red wine.

We were giddy, like schoolgirls out on their own for the first time. Estelle was thoroughly in love with our waiter, a tall string-bean of an Englishman, blond and shy and obviously enjoying us thoroughly. I was in love with our meal, with the heavy silverware and the beautiful presentation, with the wine that brought an even deeper glow to my already rosy cheeks, with the tiny lamb chops, grilled kidneys, and plump, short sausages on my plate. As we lingered over dessert, the waiter brought us a complimentary after-dinner liqueur, setting it down almost apologetically and backing away from the table shyly. We paid our bill and left, insecure about having only five dollars left between us but confident, somehow, that luck was on our side. We made the short walk to North Beach and spent the night laughing and dancing and talking to strangers, who often stopped to watch us as we walked by, one of them commenting, excusing himself first for the intrusion, that he couldn't resist telling us how beautiful we were, that we lit up the street with our glow. And we were somehow both aware of it, aware of some special quality passing through us that had nothing to do with how we looked and everything to do with how we felt, how dazzled we were by the world that night, by San Francisco, by the full moon that by then hung high over the city, our golden chaperone.

As the night wound down to what we thought would be its conclusion, we made the walk up Washington Street to Powell, where we figured we would have to walk the several blocks to my car. Safety was not a concern then, in part because it was entirely safe, in most parts of San Francisco, to walk—two women, or a woman alone—at any time, and in part because we were invincible, untouchable in our charmed circle of gold. As we reached the top of the hill, we saw the last cable car of the night headed towards the barn, empty except for the driver and conductor, the same one who had started us on our journey several hours earlier. He saw us, too, and held the car until we could hop on. Instead of heading back to the barn immediately, they offered to take us to my car and in the process gave Estelle and me our own personal cable car excursion. I was sitting alone on the outside bench, soaking up all that golden moonlight, when I looked back at Estelle and our conductor. His name is Joe, I suddenly thought to myself, almost as if someone had whispered his name. I even turned, startled, but I was alone in the moonlight in the cool San Francisco night.

By the time we reached my car, none of us wanted the night to end. Estelle and I agreed to accompany our new friends to the cable car barn and then head back to The Coachman for a drink. "By the way," the conductor said, reaching a hand towards mine, "I'm Joe." I jumped and as our eyes met, something bright and hot arced in the air between us and I looked away, flushed and out of breath. I became quieter then, letting Estelle steer the conversation, relying on her vibrancy to carry the energy of the night.

While Joe counted his receipts and changed out of his uniform, Estelle and I played ping pong. The cable cars were tucked away in their covered ports, and never have I felt more privy to the secret inside of San Francisco. Cable cars, their image, their song, the sound of their bells, make up some of my earliest memories. I love the ride from downtown, especially the first glimpse of the bay as you come over the hill. I love the creaking way they struggle up a hill, occasionally backsliding and sending a car full of terrified tourists into the oncoming traffic. And here I was behind the scenes, in Santa's workshop, control central, the very heartbeat of the city. We had just enough time left to make it to The Coachman and share a hot brandy before closing time. Joe's partner on the cable car was long gone, and it was clear by then that the alchemy was between the three of us. We climbed into Joe's car and headed west, where we sat and talked until the full

Cable car

moon sank down behind the towers of the Golden Gate Bridge and the eastern sky began to glow.

As moonlight streamed into the car like a fourth presence, Joe told Estelle to turn and look at me. "She looks like she's made out of gold, doesn't she, spun gold?" he asked, as he moved my hair out of my eyes and turned my face to the side. I was embarrassed, but I felt the glow, too, we all did; we all seemed spun out of some magical, golden fiber there in the shimmering predawn San Francisco. Reluctantly, Estelle and I said good-bye to our new friend and headed back towards the Lakeville dawn.

School was out a few weeks later and Estelle went back to Southern California for the summer. I rode the cable cars often and finally, as I knew I would, I saw Joe. I rode with him all night and when he was through counting his receipts, we went to The Coachman's Bar, this time just the two of us. When it closed, we went for a long walk down to the bay, where Joe kissed me for the first of many times and told me he loved me.

It's been a long time since I've seen Joe, longer still since I've seen or talked to Estelle. I have no idea where either of them are. At Sonoma State, there are no longer any buildings that pay homage to Edgar Allen Poe. The Coachman and The Oak Tree are both gone. The hills of Lakeville are filling with sprawling, luxury housing. It's been a long time since I wore a yellow dress and I don't remember the last time the air shimmered with so much golden possibility between me and a charming stranger. But I occasionally enjoy a good mixed grill, something I can do entirely on my own without the cooperation of the gods, and red wine still brings a soft glow to my cheeks, and for that I am very, very glad.

★

Michele Anna Jordan is a chef as well as a writer. She has written for numerous national publications, including Appellation, Bon Apetit, Food & Wine, *and* Wine Enthusiast, *and has published fifteen books, winning numerous awards along the way. Currently, she is the weekly food columnist for Sonoma County's* Press Democrat, *and she is the North Bay restaurant critic for the* San Francisco Chronicle *as well as for* San Francisco Magazine.

DAVID ROBINSON

. * .

Lunch at Pensione Suisse

It's not just food that's served here.

AT PENSIONE SUISSE, WE ALWAYS MAKE SURE WE WAKE UP IN TIME
for lunch. As I swing open the heavy shutters, the hot Neapolitan
sun, already high in the sky, floods the bare room with its brilliance.
I quickly wash in the corner sink and join the others at the table.
Mama Mia (she is all of ours while we are in her pensione) is in
the kitchen. The sound of her voice and the smell of her food en-
twine and drift in to where we are seated expectantly at a large oval
table. I have never eaten food so good, but the true bounty of this
table is in the people seated around it. I am dining as I do every
day with the other guests of the establishment, two or three of the
women who have no customers at lunchtime, one of the six Chinese tailors taking a break from measuring American sailors, Erica,
the Swiss girl put up there by her industrialist boyfriend, and
Senor Bea, an airline official bored by ordinary hotels. We are
served by the maid, Bianca, and waiter, Antonio, better known
as Antionetta, vamping as he serves. I am here with two American friends. This is my first trip to Europe.

Except when Mama Mia enters the room, we Americans tend
to focus on the women seated at the table with us. No wonder.
Across from me is Marisa, a back-alley bombshell with light flaxen

135

hair. She has a wonderful body, full and fleshy, which even in re-
pose radiates sensuality. I watch her lips and observe the lingering
traces of red she leaves when she eats an apple or smokes a cigarette. I can distinguish hers among all the other butts in the
overflowing tray. I don't know her story; why anyone is here is
pointless to ask. But even when Marisa is lounging at the table in
a simple house dress, I see her as a sophisticated lady. She could
be a star for me in any environment. She has a baby girl, around
18 months old, blonde and adorable, who looks just like Marisa
must have. There is no father; the father would be a guess, maybe
not even a memory. It's not clear what happens to the baby when
she entertains, and I never get up the nerve to find out.

Next to me is the Sicilian without a name, just Number Two
(her room). There is nothing subtle or sophisticated about Number
Two. Everything about her is black, her hair, her dresses, her
moods, a perpetual storm cloud. Another great body pushing out
at every seam, she leaves an imprint of flesh behind as other
women leave a scent. Anna Magnagni in "The Rose Tattoo" pales
by comparison. I could play her Burt Lancaster. Provocative, hot,
passionate in even the smallest gesture, Number Two flaunts her
sexuality and dares you to do something about it. At the table she
leers and cracks jokes in dialect which I don't understand but the
meaning of which is unmistakable. One day after lunch, I accept
her dare and knock on her door. She yanks open the door, looks
me up and down, laughs a loud 'Ha!' and slams it shut. She doesn't
do charity. Soon everyone in the pensione knows; there are no
secrets here. Some of the other girls, hearing about this episode
and seeing a chance, offer themselves, but burned once, I decline
another humiliation.

Sonia is the plainest of the lot and therefore the easiest to be
with. In comparison to Marisa and Number Two, she appears un-
complicated, even dull. She has only an average body which she
doesn't bother to flaunt. Sonia seems happy with life's simple pleasures like the picnics we take together in the countryside. She is
memorable for defending Mussolini and his terror with the simple
logic that only those who deserved to die died and all who died

deserved to. She doesn't allow complicated matters to trouble her. Thus, I find it hard to reconcile the stories I hear about Sonia with Sonia herself.

It must be Senor Bea, the only one at Pensione Suisse with any sense of history, who tells us that Sonia "in her youth" had "made a fortune" in Argentina. In her youth? She's still in her twenties. "Doing what?" I ask naively, which produces much guffawing around the table. In silence then, I wonder about the dimensions of this reputed fortune, how much could it have been, what might have happened to it. Sonia herself never speaks of Argentina.

Stories about Sonia emerge in her absence. We learn Sonia has a boyfriend—in fact she has two boyfriends—and that her life is not so placid after all, because one boyfriend loves her, she loves the other and the first is jealous enough to come spying. It's hard to imagine jealousy in the context of Pensione Suisse—what does the jealous lover think is going on here anyhow?—and Sonia in particular doesn't seem to inspire jealousy. But Carlo, from a well-to-do family and desperately in love, lavishes money on Sonia which she in turn bestows on the man she truly desires, Attilio. Thus Sonia continues to make and spend her fortune.

Eva is the oldest, fat and gap-toothed, but she has landed a U.S. soldier who she swears to my obvious incredulity wants to marry her. A northerner and in Naples only after years of working the small towns where supposedly she was regarded as something of a star, she is now definitely teetering over the hill, rescued just in time by the American. He comes by almost every evening. The two of them sit side by side on two chairs in the darkened hall outside her room for hours holding hands and saying nothing. He speaks no Italian, she no English. It seems to me the language of love must have its limitations. After a certain amount of hand holding, they adjourn to the bedroom to cap the evening, and later he leaves. She gets up to join us for lunch. This routine leaves Eva lots of free time during the afternoon to play cards, talk or whatever. She is not above having other men or making a pass at me when we are in the same room, although I take care to make sure we are never alone. She reaches for me across the large bed where Sonia and a group of us are playing cards, but I have the image of being chased by a cow across a field, and I scramble free.

I do not escape the clutches of the harridans who wait below on the street, nor do I particularly want to. I have been conditioned by living for weeks in the Pensione Suisse; sex is in the food, in the Neapolitan air. It permeates every part of one's being. After a while, I feel that I will burst open at any moment. That this desire has nothing to do with love shocks me at first.

My one attempt with Number Two aside, I am still shy and keep my new family off limits. The women working the street all know me and surround me every time I step out the door. Naples is renowned for the earthiness of its street walkers who blanket the city. The ones outside Pensione Suisse have been pushed back to this poor neighborhood where their clientele is mostly local, the husband out for a cigarette or the passing worker. After several glasses of wine one night I figure why not and take one of the old women upstairs. I put the weightless ten lire coin in the jerky elevator, and we slip past the somnolent doorman into my bed. The morning after on the street below, she ribaldly shouts her triumph at me for all the rest of the women to applaud, and I don't mind. It even gets easier. But one night the doorman, Peppino, wakes and spreads the word in the pensione.

Peppino is happy to be of use, delighted suddenly to have a new story to tell. He too has somehow landed at Pensione Suisse, old and spent. Unlike the rest, he revels in the past, with repetitious tales of Ethiopia where he claims to have been an important Fascist official during the Italian occupation. With his discovery of my exploits, we are linked, and he begins to treat me like a new friend. After several nights, the old woman, my lover, takes to reaching into my pockets on the street, grabbing loose change or whatever else she can put her hands on, and still I don't care. Upstairs, life goes on too.

It is called Pensione Suisse because Mama Mia's husband is Swiss. One look at the two of them gives you the whole picture, but the image that comes to mind also makes you blink. He is a fraction of her size and could be a heroic mountaineer scaling the heights of Mount Mama, but while the scale is apt, the personality is not. He is too wizened and submissive. Pensione Suisse is his Blue Angel, Mama Mia his Marlena. One can guess how the two met. It is his money that bought the pensione, but it is his and Swiss in name only. Mama Mia runs the place and everything in it and endows all with her vast, embracing Neapolitan personality. When visible at all, Senor Suisse—no one calls him anything else —sits hunched at the front desk talking to Peppino or doing the accounts. He never eats lunch with us.

Mama Mia herself was in the same business she now oversees when she was young and so too her daughter, Lela, who often comes to visit with her small son and scrawny husband. Lela has exquisite white skin set off by jet black hair and the fluffy pale sweaters she favors. Soft and plump, she, like Mama Mia must have been, is a beauty. It's not clear whether she is still working or has retired fully to family life, but Lela would fit right in at Pensione Suisse, and I have no trouble picturing her joining us at lunch or in other activities, no trouble at all.

The back windows look out on the popular quarters, rabbit warrens of old apartments crammed with the poor of Naples. There is a street market below, and food for lunch is hoisted up each day in a basket lowered from the kitchen window. We eat incredibly well. We always have fresh fruits and vegetables, and good meats too. Anything but fresh pasta would be a scandal. It is Mama Mia who does all the marketing and the cooking and supervises the staff. Leaning out the window, she shouts down her orders and her imprecations lest any vender try to overcharge her or give her less than their highest quality at their lowest price. All the negotiations of the bazaar are conducted by shouting back and forth. Even six stories below, her presence is felt. When she leans out the kitchen window, we are on the safe side of a blast furnace.

The kitchen is the center of Mama Mia's domain, and everyone comes there if they need to talk to her. The business of the pensione is conducted in the kitchen, and her desk is the chopping block behind which she stands while preparing the food for lunch. I have never seen her sitting down. Emotional and volatile, she is an Etna of a woman given to frequent eruptions. She can be scathing, and her denunciations are accompanied by a full panoply of Italian gesture. To be next to her when she is working with a knife in her hand is to risk evisceration over even a minor point of dispute. Like the others, we are wise enough to stand respectfully clear.

We are often joined at the table by other guests in the pensione. Pasquale is the youngest of the six Chinese tailors living there. (He was born in Portuguese Goa, hence the unusual name). He has fallen rapturously in love with Marisa's baby girl—if not with Marisa herself. Pasquale adores playing with the baby and gives Marisa money, a lot of money it is rumored around the table, for the baby as well as for herself. Marisa has conquered with her baby, as well as with her body, but in Naples, any survival is okay. There never could be a debate here about ends justifying the means. Life is unblinkingly amoral. The other Chinese keep to themselves and pass up Mama Mia's food for their own which they cook on hot plates in their back rooms. They go out every day to the U.S. ships to sell made-to-order suits and do a booming business. It's not clear what they think of Marisa or of Pasquale's entanglement.

Erica, the Swiss, has been stashed here by her industrialist boyfriend to keep her handy but out of sight of his family. She doesn't seem to mind the arrangement. Tall, blonde and very good looking, she seems a cut above the rest, but she is just as dependent on the desires of a man as are the others, and any class distinctions fade in the face of this common reality. She has a friendly disposition and accompanies Sonia and us on our picnics. Her boyfriend, Rudi, a Swiss-Italian, calls for her in the evenings. No friend of the working class, he runs a large family-owned tomato processing plant and has nothing good to say about the hundreds of southern Italian workers he employs. He likes to tell us of their scandalous transgressions and how many he has "had to" fire. No one in this working class pensione challenges his views, not because he is a man, although that is appreciated, not because he is rich, although that too is appreciated, but simply because that is who he is and what he thinks. Pensione Suisse is all-accepting and can afford no moralists or crusaders.

Each of the women at Pensione Suisse seems to have found herself some sort of male benefactor: Marisa, Erica, Sonia, Eva, Mama Mia, Lela, all except the outrageously independent Number Two. These women know men inside out and seem to have a very clear-headed attitude toward them and their usefulness. Neither cynical nor romantic, they are above all else, practical; only Sonia seems to lose her head in love. These women seek men not for romance but for security, in whatever form and for whatever duration it may occur.

Senor Bea has the appearance of a gentleman, refined, reserved and elegant. He is the only other man included at lunch, and he eats with us only when he can get off work. He says he prefers the atmosphere of Pensione Suisse to other hotels (as do we) for its vitality. Although he is a senior executive at the airport, he seems totally at ease in the world of Pensione Suisse. From Senor Bea, we get an education of another sort. He is well-read and speaks fluent English, and after lunch, we linger over coffee in long discussions with him about literature, history, politics and philosophy. He says he is a socialist—the only one I've ever met.

He also knows the gossip about those around the table and is not above slipping us delicious morsels from time to time. He and Bianca act as the court jesters and between them provide such oral history of the realm as exists. Apart from their stories, it's not always clear how we come to know all we know about our companions at Pensione Suisse. We observe and listen, we pick up clues in the swirl of conversation and constant bantering, but there are seldom explicit remountings and almost never anything said about the past. The women here do not sit around the table talking to one another of previous experiences. We Americans are never asked about our lives in the U.S. or about our parents or hometowns or what we do. There are no childhood reminiscences offered us either, no tales of family, work or past exploits. We understand not to ask. Even if everyone here has a past, no one has a history. Life begins afresh each day.

Sometimes the pensione takes in temporary boarders, and then they too join us for lunch. Innocents can get quite a shock. One day, an American couple, Kansas tourists, come to table with no idea of what they are getting into, but Number Two makes sure they are properly indoctrinated. The only common language she needs is a banana. The husband shows some signs of interest—he'd have to be brain dead not to—but the wife hustles him out of there fast. I don't think they even finish their soup.

Unexpectedly one day I run into another friend from college who had just docked in Naples aboard a U.S. navy ship. I invite him back to lunch at the pensione, and after several months at sea, he has no trouble appreciating the bounty of the table. After indulging in what is for us a typical four course meal, he expresses interest in some further indulgence and Marisa, understanding the situation, is willing. With Eva's intervention, the five of us set about haggling, negotiating the issue of how much for what until finally an accommodation is reached. It takes all of us half an hour around the table to arrange what left to the two of them would have taken a couple of minutes. But we feel proud of ourselves, satisfied to think that in the process we have become a little bit Neapolitan. Our friend reports satisfaction, so we are doubly pleased. I forget to ask him about the baby.

We also have temporary show-biz guests eating with us from time to time. One is Aida, a former Miss Greece, who is appearing in Naples' clubs. Tall, dramatic and classically proportioned, I think she sings, but if so, probably nobody pays much attention to her voice. Around the table, she is as haughty in her house dress as she is in her nightclub outfit, revealing and remote at the same time. She gives us postcards of herself in costume, one long taut leg thrust forward, and I keep her card on my bureau. We are also joined by the Sugar Sisters for a week or so, two innocent-looking dyed-blonde Italians trying to sing American songs they can't understand. They have been performing by trying to mimic as best they could the sounds picked up from the radio or records. None of us can carry a tune, but we undertake to tutor them in the meaning and pronunciation of the rock and roll lyrics that we know so well, and after lunch they rehearse with us. It's hard to get through a line without cracking up. We never catch their show at the nightclub, but we know it by heart by the time they leave.

Bianca, the maid who knows all, keeps no secrets. She is rosy-cheeked, cheerful and tiny in her blue uniform dress, wry and direct in her humor, shrewd and caustic in her observations. She skewers everyone—with the judicious exception of Mama Mia—but without malice. Thanks principally to Bianca, we know something about everyone's character, their quirks or preferred indulgences—especially sexual—and all this information is available to be used by anyone in conversation or in the frequent verbal jousting that goes on around the table. Bianca can be self-deprecating as well. One day she asks me if I would consider marrying her daughter. I say my Italian isn't good enough for me to talk to her. She tells me not to worry—all I have to say is 500 lire. Everyone—for this is at the table too—roars.

Antonio wears a white waiter's coat. He helps Bianca serve lunch and does the dishes afterwards. Antonio sashays as he serves, speaking in a high-pitched voice with the full range of exaggerated effeminate gestures. Everyone calls him Antoinetta, which he prefers. He seems to love his role; he adores being teased by the women and gives it back as fast and as strong as he gets it. His long brown hair is slicked back and held in place with bobby pins, and he hikes his apron like a skirt. Antonio is a good twenty years ahead of his time. One wonders what it must be like for him out on the streets of Naples. But it is clear that Pensione Suisse is a sanctuary for him (as well as for us) and here he is free to be who he wants to be. His job is not dependent on pretending to be something he's not. In this environment, any pretense would be punctured quickly, most likely by one of Bianca's deft barbs. But more than that, he is frank about his preferences and, at Pensione Suisse he has an accepting audience in front of which he can discuss his love problems.

Antoinetta has fallen madly in love with a newly married man who just moved in with his wife across the narrow street. When their shutters are open, he can see into their apartment. He has taken to frequenting the balcony opposite their apartment hoping to be noticed. In a fit of desperate inspiration, he borrows a dress from Sonia and prances flirtatiously on the balcony in an effort to draw the newlywed's interest but to no avail. Unusual for Pensione Suisse, Antoinetta's desires remain unfulfilled.

In the afternoons we often go out to explore Naples, to sit and soak up the afternoon sun, to read and talk while we digest the meal and the events of the table. Two or three months pass, the pace of our lives has changed. We have glimpsed another world, one normally inaccessible to outsiders. We dream about staying in Naples, maybe going into business, maybe even running a place like Pensione Suisse where we could have all the pleasures of our own table and create our own family around it. We debate how best to do this but without any resolution. Finally, we decide we'll come back to Naples after we first visit some other places in Europe which we have wanted to see. With this agreed upon, we come to the decision to leave Naples in order to continue our travels. With great effort, we rouse ourselves and say goodbye to Mama Mia and all the others.

Our last lunch is like every lunch, wonderful, bountiful, entertaining. Leaving is sad for us, for we will miss them all, but we know that life at Pensione Suisse will go on as usual without much reference to us. Unlike us, tomorrow will bring them no nostalgic memories of today.

★

David Robinson is a photographer whose first book was a photo essay on Italy. Since living at Pensione Suisse he has returned to Italy over twenty times. He has published six books of his photographs plus numerous articles on photography and travel. Two of his recent books are on European cemeteries: Saving Graces *and* Beautiful Death. *After twenty-five years in Boston, he and his wife now live in Mill Valley, California.*

* ✳ *

Treading Water

Change can be glacial, but glaciers
are made of water.

I'D NEVER SEEN ANYTHING LIKE IT. THE SURFACE OF PUGET SOUND boiled with turbulence, then was calm as a pond. One minute waves rocked the kayak and I had to brace with the paddle, the next minute the surface seemed pocked with rain. Ahead, the waves ripping the sea looked like a river dropping into rapids, to the left and right, upwellings belched like the breath of serpents.

I'd never been so low to the water on a body so large and animated, but at that moment on the Sound I understood for the first time that the sea is alive. Its personalities were popping up all around me. I watched the surface with every paddle-stroke, reading the currents, anticipating the waves, riding up one side of a swell and down the other, concentrating, always concentrating. The black clouds overhead threatened rain or worse, but the sea was still friendly and I was cautious but not afraid. We had just another mile to the safe harbor of Turn Island, and I was optimistic we'd get there in time.

My mind shifted to a small lake in Minnesota, in the warm sun of summertime. Blue dragonflies glinted like jewels as they alighted on the edge of the boat. Lily pads sparkled. The lake shimmered. Everything was glassy and brilliant and fresh. I loved the dragonflies but was anxious that they'd bite, and my five-year-old mind couldn't formulate the questions or understand the anxiety as my father silently fished. There were air bubbles in the paint on the rowboat's planks, and when I poked one with my finger my father warned, "Be careful, if you break that the boat will leak." How numerous the air bubbles seemed, how fragile the boat, how far away the shore. I hardly dared to move.

When I was growing up it seemed every winter we'd hear on the radio or read in the paper a story about another accident on a frozen lake. The ice should have been thick enough to support a car, but one went down anyway taking a family to their deaths. My child's mind couldn't express the fear I felt when we went ice-fishing and my parents drove the car out onto the frozen surface. They were always cautious, and I knew they'd never do anything to put us at risk. But every winter I heard the stories.

I never really thought about my fear of water. It was something that existed, had mass and weight and reality like a mountain or a meadow. Others somehow weren't afraid, and it just seemed to me that their reality and mine were different and unchangeable in the way that you couldn't change your height, your freckles, or the color of your eyes.

I wasn't eager to take my first swimming lesson, but I think it had as much to do with my older brothers' lack of enthusiasm as my own. Mornings in Minnesota in early June can be cool, and the few lessons I did take were awful. We spent so much time shivering on the pool deck in the morning breeze that when we were told to get into the water it was something I could hardly bear. I learned only that swimming lessons were painful and my parents mercifully allowed us to stop after two or three. As it turned out this might have been a mistake, but it's impossible to say because without better conditions we may never have learned the value and joy of swimming anyway.

Like me, my brothers Bruce and Gene couldn't swim. We never talked about it as we grew older, but I think they felt more or less the same as I. We were filling our lives with other things, dreaming other dreams. Water played little role in our plans.

When I was 16, I was the youngest player on a baseball team. We were playing our way toward the state championship but facing a strong team in a divisional championship game, and I was called on to pitch. I pitched well on that hot August day, but not well enough and we lost a close game. The loss ended our season and I was soaking in the bathtub at home, feeling despondent, when I heard my father on the phone in the kitchen and from the tone of his voice I knew there had been a far greater loss that day.

I never got the whole story. I always imagined Gene reaching too far out with the paddle, maybe pointing at something, maybe reaching for a stronger stroke. I don't know why I always saw it this way, but I also always wondered if he'd ever been in a canoe before. I don't think he had been, don't think he understood how unstable they can be. I also never completely understood how it affected me, but in my sleep I could feel his fear, his panic, the terror of knowing he couldn't escape; I could feel his suddenly slow slide into unconsciousness and death. It terrified me, and I don't remember when I first got in the water again after Gene drowned.

To graduate from Dartmouth I had to pass a swim test or take a year of swim classes. That requirement is probably long gone now but it was good for me. It got me into a class that wasn't completely awful, the first such experience I'd had. I learned that I could do an elementary backstroke and continue to breathe, and I could jump into just about any depth of water if I planned my escape and knew how to get there. But I didn't come out of the class comfortable with water.

Some years later I was planning an extended trip around the world and something told me that I would face death before I returned. Somehow I knew that death would come to me in the form of water. Was it a warning from Gene? A vision of another destiny I shared with the brother who shared my childhood? I didn't know, but I hired a private instructor in San Francisco to teach me to swim. She worked with me for several sessions, helped me a little, but, like others before her, couldn't get at the root of my fear. Nor could I. My only model for overcoming problems was to push through them. I'd been a successful athlete since I was a boy and all the coaching I'd received stressed fighting through obstacles. I didn't understand the subtleties of finesse. So I left for Southeast Asia with death by water lurking in the back of my mind.

I tested it in many places: body surfing at Kuta Beach in Bali, swimming in Lake Toba in Sumatra, snorkeling at Koh Samui in Thailand. Never was I quite comfortable, and my next attempt at snorkeling in Trincomalee, Sri Lanka, was different.

I was traveling with a Canadian and a New Zealander, new friends discovered on the world travelers' circuit who were heading my direction for a time. Together we made our way to Trincomalee on the eastern side of the island, and in time we found snorkeling gear to rent and a place to wade into the sea. We scouted it from the rocks above and I didn't like what I saw. Waves rolled in and broke over successive reefs of coral, creating rows of shallows and depths and lots of froth. I couldn't see any easy way in or out, and my anxieties began to build.

Nick and Tracey were ready to go but I couldn't do it. I couldn't see my way out once in, and the tightness in my chest made breathing difficult.

"I'll wait and watch from here. Go ahead without me." It was the best I could do.

They made their way down to the beach, entered the surf, and gradually swam farther out, timing the waves and moving gingerly over the rocks and coral. The waves pushed them around, but in time they got to calm water and explored the depths, diving, coming up to the surface, blowing streams of water out their snorkels, enjoying themselves. I watched and waited, but the tightness in my chest remained. Sometime later they came out, again moving cautiously over the rocks and coral as the surf shoved them around, then walked up the beach toward me.

We decided to try another spot, some distance away, and when we got there it was more to my liking. The sea was calm, settled blue and deep and tranquil in a wide, protected bay. The rocks dropped down to the water and I could see an easy way in and out, at the backside of a rocky arm that protruded into the sea and acted as a natural breakwater. It would take little to climb down, ease my way in, and pull myself out when ready.

Tracey and Nick went first, swam out from the rocks, and soon all I could see were the humps of their backs, snorkels bobbing on the surface.

The first plunge is always the most difficult, and my chest constricted as I got in and felt the cool water against my skin. A short breath, then another, and another: the snorkel was working; I could breathe. I pushed myself away from the rocks, breathed nervously, paddled my feet to keep myself afloat and the snorkel above the surface. The sound echoed in my head, and the sound of air coursing through that plastic pipe was the sound of life, the sound of my survival.

I saw many things, but only with a fragment of my awareness. Most of my attention was on my snorkel, on the sound of my breathing, on the need to keep the snorkel above the surface.

My mask had a poor seal and began to fill with water. Many times I'd seen friends empty their masks while treading water, blow out their snorkels, and continue. I couldn't do this. My life depended on being able to breathe, and I didn't have the courage to tilt my head back willfully, empty my mask, and risk dropping my snorkel below the surface and losing my lifeline while I tried to tread water. I simply could not do it. But I was prepared, having planned my exit from the sea. I moved to the rocks, grabbed hold with one hand, emptied my mask with the other, then pushed away again and resumed breathing through the snorkel.

Sunlight shimmered through the sea, lighting up neon-colored fish. I paddled around on the surface, careful to remain near the rocks because my mask began to fill again. The salt water burned my eyes, and I had to repeat the procedure for emptying my mask: grab the rocks, empty the mask, replace it, head down, push away, breathe.

The third time I did this I noticed that Tracey and Nick were far away, out in the middle of the bay. I felt a momentary embarrassment that I wasn't out there with them, but that wasn't where my reality lay. Near the rocks I could fix my equipment, and I could continue to breathe.

When I went back out that time I noticed a new motion in the water. I sensed a gradual rising and falling, and I began to get splashes of water in my snorkel, surprising drafts of seawater inhaled with my precious air that sent jolts of adrenaline through my body. The next time I went to the rocks to empty my mask, a swell carried me up a couple of feet along the rocks and settled me back down again. This was new.

The sea continued to move, gradually up, then down. My mask continued to fill, faster than before. Now when I went to the rocks the swells carried me higher, then dropped me lower. I had to push myself firmly away from the rocks to avoid being scraped down them like soft cheese on a grater. Back in the water I sensed I had to get out, but I had drifted a short distance from my exit point. My mask was filling fast and I needed to empty it. This time the swell took me high up the rocks and dropped me hard along their sharp surface, scraping off bits of flesh, sending dull pains through my hip. My breathing was quick now. Coming in frantic bursts. My mask was still full of water. My eyes were burning, my vision blurred. I had to empty my mask, find my way to the safe exit point.

Back to the rocks again, rising with the swells, being scraped down the rocks like driftwood. At the trough of the wave I was able to clear the mask, then pushed away from the rocks. Breathing again, swimming now, toward the exit. But suddenly a force threw me backward and water rushed into my lungs. Gone. No air now, no breath, no lifeline, only one way out. The snorkel had come apart at the seams, leaving the mouthpiece wedged between my teeth in a bite forged by fear. But it was useless with the pipe disconnected, tangled now in the straps of my mask. I tried not to breathe, to keep the water out, but the panic forced me to inhale. Water, no air, just water burning my lungs, my eyes, my consciousness.

Suddenly I had a gasp of air. I'd surfaced. I kicked with all my strength toward the exit, toward the rocks where I'd entered, riding the rising swell toward land, toward air, toward the breath of life. I reached out with both hands and grabbed hold to pull myself out. But I was blasted head-on by a force almost too strong to resist. Water ripped my head back, poured into my mouth, tore one hand off the rocks and tugged at my body like a demon trying to drag me into darkness. All my strength, every electron of my awareness went into that one hand holding that rock, one finger now, just the fingertip clawing onto the rock against the force of that torrent. My whole being knew that I would be lost if that fingertip lost its grip, that I'd be swept into a vortex with no hope of escape.

It went on for an eternity, but finally the pressure abated, the water withdrew, the fingertip held. I scrambled out onto the rocks on rubber legs, gasping hysterically, stumbling this way and that, my motor functions stripped by the hormones of panic. Higher. I had to get higher. Away from the water. Higher, still higher. I could hardly walk, could hardly breathe. I fell, and fell again, scraping myself on sharp stones, climbing blindly away from the sea and certain death, knowing that I had to get far away from the water where it couldn't follow.

Finally I collapsed, exhausted, frightened beyond description, only raising my head once to see my two friends still paddling around in the sea, marveling at the sights beneath the surface. My breath came in gasps and all the images of Gene's death flooded back, images now hopelessly mixed with my own. But I was still here. I was still alive.

It's impossible to describe such panic to anyone who hasn't experienced it. Every synapse, every cell in the body gets infected by it, and I don't know how long it takes to work it out.

I have experienced nothing so debilitating as this raw terror. And whenever it happened after that afternoon I would descend into the depths of despair. Every ounce of confidence would drain from my body and my sense of self-worth would evaporate. My usual optimism would sometimes take only a few hours to return, but sometimes days, or weeks.

I didn't know how to change my reality. Much of my life was ruled by this tension between my grounded, confident self, and the paralyzed, helpless being I became when confronted with water. I refused to be daunted, refused to miss out on experiences I wanted to have, but equally was incapable of building my own skills to make having these experiences a safe and pleasant pursuit. I tried to fight through it, again and again.

Before I went off to raft the Zambezi River I visited a psychic healer hoping to find a key to unlock the fear I carried with me every day. She spoke to me and read the responses in my body as I lay on her table, going back over some of the key experiences in my history. She said she saw me with a close friend, on a river in Africa, two 19th-century missionaries crossing in a small boat. The friend was my brother in this life, and he'd come back to help me out. I died on that river, not by drowning, but by crocodiles when the boat capsized. My friend lived. And became my brother, Gene, who died a hundred years later.

The Zambezi River is crawling with crocodiles, and the guides gave us a talk before we set out that chilled me to the bone. They were sober, clear and direct about the dangers. The river was huge and completely wild. Many of the rapids were Class V; some were unrunnable. Rafts would flip. We'd have only ourselves to rely on. "This is not about being macho," one said. "We'll be out of contact with the outside world for three days. We're not trying to freak you out. But if you have any doubts about this trip, back out now. This is your last chance, and no one will think you're a coward."

I had grave doubts. Could I last a week on one of the world's wildest rivers, running rapid after rapid in crocodile-infested waters? My gut told me no, but my rational mind said yes. When I saw the river up close I had to sit down and compose myself. The power of that water plunging from Victoria Falls, then racing down the narrow channel and ripping through a canyon of basalt was greater than anything I'd ever seen. When the first raft set out and snapped an oar at the first rapid, I should have left. But I didn't, and for once, my way of dealing with things head-on worked. We made our way downriver for a week, riding wild rapids but never capsizing or losing anyone overboard.

Two years later I wasn't so lucky. On a tributary of the Tembeling River in the heart of the Malaysian jungle, we were swimming beneath a small waterfall. There were numerous deep pools out of the current where I could leap in and get out without worry. But many of the group were swimming across the narrow river to a pool on the other side, and friends convinced me it would take only two or three good strokes to get there. I had my doubts, knowing that if I didn't make it before the current took me downstream I'd lose my safe exit and then I'd enter unknown territory. But three of them said they'd swim alongside me and help if I had trouble.

My strokes weren't strong enough, probably because of my fear. I got only halfway across before the current took me past the landing point and panic struck. I was immobilized, helpless, with three friends shoving me up to keep my head above water. Somewhere downstream they pushed me toward shore and I was able to grab the branches of an overhanging tree and get my footing, but I was devastated again. Confidence shattered, I sat in the sand trying to get my breath, and to understand the fear that steals my strength. My friends, too, were quiet, startled by this transformation. We were equally lost in this mystery of my psyche.

Later, when I had the opportunity to learn to scuba dive I faced the same old fears. I'd done a one-day walk-in scuba course in the Virgin Islands and had no fear of being submerged as long as I could breathe, and scuba gear didn't frighten me, but to go through the training, to sink beneath the surface, this was another matter.

The intensive scuba certification course we took in the Philippines gave me a whole new level of confidence in the water, and in fact, the only part that scared me was when I had to take off my tank and pass it up to the boat at the end of the dive. Again, my guarantee of air was essential to my comfort, and without it fear crept into every crevice. I managed to get through that and soon found myself enthralled by the depths.

But certified or not, I still couldn't leap into water that was over my head unless I had a sure way out. I couldn't tread water, and couldn't keep myself afloat except in the most benign of circumstances.

It was almost by chance that I saw an ad for a seminar at an outdoors fair in San Francisco: Swimming for Adults Afraid in Water. Was I afraid in water? Could I say no and look myself in the eye? It took me a while to take the step, but eventually I decided to drop in and see what the woman teaching the seminar had to say.

I was surprised at the number of people who came to hear Melon Dash speak. There were at least twenty. Were all of these people afraid in water? Melon spoke with calm, reassuring tones, and asked us to do a few exercises with her, to go back into our pasts and try to recall the very first time we were afraid in water, back to an experience when someone or something brought fear or anxiety into our lives, or when we brought it into ourselves unknowingly. I've never been very good at this sort of memory mining, and I never really got to any first experience, but after a while she asked people to talk about what they remembered. The stories were fascinating.

Few were similar except for the final result, that something in the experience had been connected to a paralyzing fear of being in water. The longer I sat there and the more stories I listened to the more I was convinced that she was on to something. I signed up.

Melon's teaching is simple at its core. She works with small groups, provides exercises to explore the source of our fears in water, encourages us to share these experiences with others, and emphasizes having fun. Never, at any time, should you do anything in the water that isn't fun. As soon as it's no longer fun, you stop, and go back to whatever you were doing that was fun.

Sitting beneath the surface in shallow water holding our breath until we want to come up. Lying on the pool bottom. Playing with each other. Through fun we begin to understand the dynamics of water and the human body, not through an intellectual or logical approach, but through fun. It was amazing how quickly fun translated into comfort, how quickly comfort translated into confidence, and confidence into learning.

Through incremental challenges accompanied by the mantra of

"fun," I learned that the water would support me, that breathing was not difficult, that the water and I were of the same elements, that I could be comfortable and unafraid in water.

In six short weeks under Melon's tutelage I undid forty years of battles. There's no secret to it, no overwhelming challenge, no great epiphany—well, there were several small epiphanies, to be sure—I just needed to be guided by someone who knew how to help.

Near the end of my course I was at a convention in Puerto Vallarta, and a friend and I needed to escape the stifling conference rooms so we ran out to the sea. We swam out past the breakers and talked about our lives and careers, friends and families, plans for the short and long term, all the while treading water in the swells. It was almost an afterthought for me, the realization that I was doing this, having a conversation in the sea in water over my head without a moment's worry. My passage had been so effortless, so gentle and so complete, that I hardly even noticed it. Melon would have understood entirely: I was just having fun. And it was only then that I realized how truly bound to my brother I was. I had resolved my fear of water as a way to resolve his death. I had learned to swim for me, but also for him.

On Puget Sound that day the sea's moods changed by the second. We paddled our kayaks through rough waters, across calm seas, over boils and swells and whirlpools. The rain came down but felt warm as it slid off us. And soon we broke into the lee of the island, and I thought of my long-lost brother, of my brushes with death and the deep-rooted fears that took so long to exorcise, that couldn't be exorcised by fighting through them, by attacking them head-on, by any technique I knew, but simply with the help of an extraordinary woman and by finding joy in the water.

The beach was only a few strokes away. We'd camp here for the night. I stopped paddling and let the kayak glide toward the sand.

I couldn't have done it without Gene's help, without Melon's help, and wherever I go they're with me, and I know we'll be paddling in together safely to harbor.

★

Larry Habegger, executive editor of Travelers' Tales, has been writing about travel since 1980. In the early '80s he co-authored mystery serials for the San Francisco Examiner *with James O'Reilly, and since 1985 their syndicated column "World Travel Watch," has appeared in five countries and on WorldTravelWatch.com. He regularly teaches the craft of travel writing at workshops and writers conferences, and he lives with his family in San Francisco.*

WENDY DUTTON

* ✱ *

The Places I Went When My Mother Was Dying

Mother Nature comforts and heals.

THESE ARE THE PLACES I WENT WHEN MY MOTHER WAS DYING. Keep in mind she had cancer, so she was dying for a long time. Also keep in mind I have two small children, so the only way I could even begin to contemplate her death was to go deep into the wilderness. Some people think I'm crazy to camp alone in remote places, but for me there's no other kind of camping. I have never had any trouble. It's all in the approach.

My first such venture was to the Warner Mountains in the upper northwest corner of California. It was the first time I camped on national land, which means you can pretty much camp anywhere, though the best place is an old cowboy camp where you can find a ring of stones for a fireplace and the whole place littered with empty beer cans. I pictured the cowboys, getting sloshed, letting the cows run rampant. Giant cowpies were everywhere—as if there had been giant cows and giant cowboys who had to drink extra beers just to get a wilderness buzz.

I didn't exactly go alone. I went with Matthew. This was his vision quest spot. His mom led people on vision quests for a living. When he was thirteen, she brought Matthew along and he went off like everyone else for three days of solitary camping—no food, just water. After that he didn't want to do any more vision quests and he developed a lifelong fetish for water, but he still liked to come to this place. It's true it was a totally alone place and therefore it had a kind of magic. Even the air there was different at such a high altitude. It sort of sparkled and had a watery taste.

I wanted to do a vision quest too, but I wanted to skip all the New Age stuff and cut right to the solitude. And so Matthew left me alone for a few days. I pictured him camped out somewhere above me, watching me gorging on granola and writing in my notebook. I even wrote at night. It was impossible to sleep with all those mosquitoes, divebombing in the moonlight. Even the mosquitoes were giant in those mountains.

On our last day we hiked so high I was dizzy. We got so high only the strongest wildflowers bloomed. "These are the Happy Mountains," Matthew informed me. "That's their real name." I skipped around like Maria in *The Sound of Music*. And then, suddenly, a view! We could see clear into Nevada. "That's the Surprise Valley," Matthew said. And it certainly was.

Whenever I went somewhere, I reported my travels to my mother. Though I write like a maniac, I never have been much of one for a journal. My mother was my journal. She was the person I told. Every time I returned from a trip, she asked me all about it over the phone. It was hard for her to imagine the far-outness of my destinations. She admired my affinity for aloneness, something she never liked.

Then she got cancer. It started out as breast cancer, her major fear. As we talked about it on the phone, and I felt my skin tingle, and my breasts ached. She told me this when I was about to leave for a trip to the dessert with Matthew. We decided to go anyway. What else was there to do?

This time Matthew didn't leave me alone, and it annoyed me, having him trip around the trickle of creek we had found, obstructing my view of nothingness. Finally he suggested we go on a rock collecting hike. He knew a trail that went to a place where there were crystals. "It's just a little bit up there," he said, "past that miner's shack."

I pictured us ambling along, picking up crystals. But "a little bit up" turned out to be several miles up, and there were no trees there, and it was sweltering hot, and our water jugs weighed us down. I felt like a kid, asking if we were there yet. But it was a long time before we were there. And when we reached the top, someone had dynamited the hilltop and scavenged all the good crystals. We took some, but there was no joy in it.

On the way down, we began to quarrel. It wasn't just the long hike—it was my mom, or more precisely my panic about my mom. Suddenly everything seemed tragic, even my relationship with Matthew, because I quickly came to realize it would not sustain me through this crisis. Some people are good to be around when you are troubled, and some people are not. When you get to that up-in-the-air place, you can see that more clearly.

"My mom can't even help me with this," I worried. "My mom has cancer. Now we will talk about cancer. Boyfriends and camping trips will seem trite by comparison. These crystals in my hand won't even matter."

In Indiana there are a lot of malls. In the winter people go to the malls to stay out of the cold. In the summer they go to the malls to stay out of the heat. You move from one air-conditioned place to the next. When I was there, we went from my mother's house to the hospital.

I read to my mom from the book I had read in the desert, *Rebecca*. I read to her through her first chemo treatment. She sat in a big "barber" chair while the toxic medicine pumped into her from an I.V. Other patients were in other chairs, and behind them was all glass and a baby woods so green it glared. I am a good reader. I skipped over the descriptions and got right to the part where the man says, "You thought I loved Rebecca! I never loved Rebecca!" Everyone was listening, even the nurses.

At my mother's house, my mother said, "Do you want to see my scar?" But she was already unbuttoning her shirt. And she showed me where her breast had been cut away. It was a deep pink line with a white star at the end of it, and my breasts began to ache again, looking at her.

"I brought you something," I murmured, and I pressed a crystal into her hand.

She fawned over it. She couldn't believe I had found it myself.

And then for a time the cancer went away. I took myself on a trip to celebrate. I wanted to go up to the Oregon border where the redwoods grow as big as houses. I wanted to get up against that kind of size and tap into some good old-fashioned humility.

In those parts the redwoods grow right up to the coastline. The constant fog and mist conceal the actual contour of the rolling cliffs. Most days the ocean is just something you guess at. It's a foggy netherland, floating out there somewhere, and the trees are its towering protectors, stout as soldiers.

I went in the spring when there were hardly any people, and I fell asleep on a hillside beneath a mammoth redwood. When I woke, it had started to rain. It was still dark, so I moved to the car. When I woke again, I realized my mistake: I had left my shoes out in the rain.

I always had one big screw-up when I was camping—like forgetting my hat or forgetting matches or forgetting my knife. Letting my shoes get wet, that was a big one. That's why I liked camping alone; there was no one to scold me. Matthew and I had split up, but I still appreciated him for showing me how to camp. I appreciate that a lot actually.

Since my shoes were wet, I hiked barefoot in the redwoods. The trails were so springy. The ferns gave off a lushness, casting huge lacy patterns in the forest. It was still rainy and my feet went numb. Sometimes I ran to keep warm. I ran from sunny spot to sunny spot. I climbed over immense fallen trees. I spotted some elk. I didn't spot any people. I was the freeest free in that forest. Then the cancer came back.

In Indiana my mother said, "Are you ready to see my head?" But she was already taking off her wig. Her head was bald and babyish, and she smiled, and then she cried because she thought I didn't like it.

The next day I stood in front of the mirror. Whenever I got to my mother's house, I looked in the mirror and thought I looked shaggy. My skin looked extra porous in her mirror, and my hair looked frayed like I had just come home after being out in the woods for a long long time. My mother came in and caught me cutting off a couple inches of my hair. "What are you doing?" she said.

The chemo didn't work. The cancer had spread to irretrievable places like the liver and the brain. The brain was the clincher. She called and told me that just before I was leaving on a trip to Mendocino for Thanksgiving. It was another escape plan, a solitude trip. I was glad to still go. I got deep into the Mendocino National Forest where there were no people whatsoever, just manzanita, pine, redwood, a shrinking lake, a noisy stream, falling rock. In the night I heard howling, and I liked it.

"Oh, I wish I could go with you," my mother had said; I felt as if she had. I felt it especially when I was driving out of the forest and along the Eel River, and I came across a bald eagle. He was sitting on a branch overlooking the river and also right next to the road. I pulled up right in front of him and got out of my truck. "You're supposed to fly away," I told him. I made like my arms were wings and flapped at him, but he held his perch boldly and let me study him. He had magnificent yellow talons, a snowy white cap, and a hooked yellow beak, dark brown body. "You're something," I told the bird. And still he wouldn't fly away. When I got back in the truck, I thought, "She's still with me."

My mother lay on the bed like she was offering herself to us, her body bloated and yellow, her head, bald and round, her expressions, so child-like. I memorized her body: her breasts not breasts at all, the stretchmarks flaring white across her belly, the bruises on her eyes, the spidery blue veins on her cinched feet. I knew she would never walk again. I knew it in an instant.

She babbled some. She spouted mathematical equations. Then she stopped talking. She had already stopped eating. They disconnected the IV, and that meant she had a couple days. But a couple days came and went, four days, five days. She lay there, staring wide-eyed, sometimes crying out. She did not die for nine days. Or was it ten?

I counted the trees outside her window. I wondered what it would all look like without snow. And when no one else was in the room, I said, "You're supposed to fly away." And I saw her in my mind's eye, flying away from me into a beautiful mountainous landscape, and then the mountains fell away, and it was just sky where she was going.

In the Spring I took my daughters to Big Sur. They were not so crazy about camping with me. That's because I didn't have a tent and had gotten in the habit of sleeping under the stars. My kids didn't like that. There are so many noises when you are sleeping on the ground. The world is alive all around you, and it can keep a kid awake, I'll tell you.

So I rented a cabin, and we woke up with the Big Sur Creek rushing at our feet. I woke before the girls and took an icy dip. The water was so cold it hurt. It had a metallic feeling, so silver and shining. I have wished many times since to start my day that way again.

I was starting to feel human again. That water could do that to you. But still it was a surprise. My mother had been dead three months, and I missed her terribly. Often I saw her face, her body, and I heard her weird dying words. And I wondered when I would remember her whole again as she had been before the cancer, my beautiful touchstone person, my mother.

That trip was all mother to me. But to my girls it was the water, the cliffs, getting naked, and running around crazily. Naturally I wanted to tell my mother about it, how beautiful my girls had looked when they rose and found me in the creek.

"What are you doing in the *water?*" they squealed.

"Breathing deeply," I replied, but they were already rushing out to meet me.

*

Wendy Dutton has published work in The Threepenny Review, Hip Mama, The Single Mother's Companion, *and* Farmer's Market. *She lives in Oakland, California, with her two daughters, where she gardens for a living.*

. ⋆ ✳ ⋆

The Pelican

A woman answers a bird's SOS.

MALIBU BEACH, BEFORE DAWN. MY FRIEND LOUISE COMAR AND I tightened our goggles and slid our feet into the surfline. For the past six months I had been coaching Louise. Today we would swim fifteen miles, from Malibu pier to the Santa Monica pier—the longest distance Louise had ever swum and the ultimate test to determine whether she would be able to reach her goal that summer: to swim across the Catalina Channel, from Catalina Island to the California mainland, about twenty-seven miles.

Swimming was a hobby for Louise. By profession, she was a deputy district attorney in Los Angeles. She was dedicated, intense, driven, and relentless in the courtroom—all attributes that easily carried over to the sport of long-distance swimming.

But swimming in ocean was completely different from the pool, and I felt very responsible for her during our training sessions, especially today. Many dangerous obstacles would not be apparent to a new open-water swimmer.

"When you go around the pier," I coached her, "swim on the outside of me and stay at least one hundred meters out so you don't get tangled in fishing lines."

She nodded. Her eyes were focused like lazers on the water, mentally rehearsing her swim as if she were about to present a case to a jury. She was wound up tight. Way too tight. If I didn't calm her down and reassure her, she would quickly burn herself out through nervous energy.

"Louise, let's put this workout into perspective," I said. "The longest you've ever swum is ten miles. We're adding five, and that's a big stretch. If you can complete even eleven or twelve miles today, you've done a great job. Just remember, whatever distance you do today will bring you closer to your goal."

Louise took a deep breath. "I understand," she said. "But I want to swim the distance."

I told her that was fine, but that she had to pace herself. "Long-distance swimming is about going the distance, but it's also about enjoying the journey."

We decided to unwind a little by watching the sunrise. Rosy light spread across the cool blue Pacific, washing over the old wooden pier and highlighting a flock of pelicans that silently glided toward us in single file and perfect formation, riding on the air current created by the breaking waves.

We dove beneath the waves, swam around Malibu pier, and paralleled the coast. As we swam south just outside the surfline, we watched the earth awaken. Sunlight poured slowly over Malibu canyon's undulating walls, saturating the soft green grasses, silver shrubs, and wild mustard in warm morning light. A breeze stirred the hillsides and carried the fragrances of sage, rosemary, and creosote mingled with rose. We drew in deep wonderful breaths and the breeze-beveled water sparkled like a zillion diamonds. Light streamed below the surface, illuminating silvery bubbles rolling rythmically off Louise's finger tips and out of her mouth. She was feeling great. She even smiled. She was precisely on pace.

Then out of the corner of my eye, I noticed something in the water. It was a young pelican, a fledgling. It was paddling directly toward me.

"I think something's wrong with that pelican," I said to Louise. "They don't usually swim with people."

The pelican moved closer. It seemed as if it were asking for my help. I swam around the bird. Surprisingly, it didn't move away. I moved closer to take a better look. I saw a fishing line tangled around its beak, breast, and wings.

If I could guide the bird to a rock, I thought, it could climb out and I could untangle it. With Louise swimming just ahead of me, I spotted a rock rising from the water. The pelican paddled right along beside me until we reached it. But when the bird tried to leap onto the narrow shelf, it flailed; its legs and feet were also tangled in fishing line. I tried to get out of the water, but the rock was covered with barnacles.

I continued swimming down the coast, searching for another rock on which to land, and the pelican followed. Louise, swimming just ahead, looked back. "What are you doing?" she shouted. She sounded annoyed.

"I'm trying to find a place to free the pelican from the fishing line," I said. I thought of going ashore with the bird, but wasn't sure I should leave Louise swimming alone. And I knew she didn't want to stop. I was torn between insuring Louise's safety and saving the pelican's life.

About a mile ahead was Las Tunas Beach. I knew Louise could swim safely there; the surf that day was less than a foot, and there were no underwater obstacles. I gave her a choice to continue swimming to Las Tunas or come ashore right then with me.

"I want to keep going," she said. "I'll be fine."

But I could tell she wasn't happy about going alone. I felt like I was letting her down, but I couldn't just let the pelican die. I turned to shore at Big Rock Beach and guided the bird in with me. The swells began lifting us four and five feet up then dropping us down again. Sensing the danger of the waves, the pelican suddenly veered away from the surfline.

If I were going to help this bird, I'd have to pull it to shore. I looked at its pouch and neck. They were covered with lice and large, black ticks; the pelican had been unable to preen itself because of the fishing line. An enormous wave rose above us and the bird started to panic. I grabbed its giant, soft beak and started swimming with one arm and kicking as fast as I could. The wave caught us and tossed us over the falls, whitewater crashing around us. I tried to hold on and keep the bird's head above water, but the wave tore it from my grip.

Desperately, I scanned the water. Finally the young pelican emerged in the surf, tumbling, completely bound and helpless, sliding in the backwash toward an oncoming wave. Sprinting toward it, I grabbed its beak and rode with it on the whitewater into the beach.

Onshore, I let the stunned pelican stand there a few moments to get over the shock of tossing in the waves. I saw it had a deep gash in its leg from the fishing line. Its whole body began to tremble and its eyes began closing, as if it were going into shock. I talked to it and told it that it would be okay. Stroking its feathers, I gently tried to open its beak.

The fishing line was tangled so tightly that I could open the beak only a few inches. But I saw a three-pronged hook imbedded inside, the fishing line attached. I tried to pull out the hook, but couldn't grip it. Clearly I couldn't save this pelican alone.

Louise was swimming just offshore. "I need your help!" I shouted.

She immediately swam into shore and jogged over to us.

"I need you to get some scissors from one of those houses up the beach so we can cut the line," I said.

Louise ran across Big Rock Beach and climbed a steep embankment. At the first house, an old woman called out that she was too frail to walk to the door. At the second house, a young woman answered from inside that she was too busy to help. At the third house, an elderly man answered, who immediately and wisely grabbed a pair of pliers and jogged with Louise down to the beach.

The pelican was going into deeper shock. The man and Louise held the pelican, who stood patiently on the sand, letting us work on him. I used the pliers to cut the lines and we carefully pulled them off its wings, breast, beak, and between its feet.

When I opened its beak to remove the hook, we saw there were two additional three-pronged hooks inside. Using the pliers, I pulled out the first one. The pelican blinked and squirmed a little, but didn't try to get away. The second hook took three attempts to yank out. The last hook was so deeply imbedded that I couldn't remove it. The man gave it a try, and in a matter of moments he pulled the last hook out.

We examined the bird's body. All the lines were gone and the hooks were out. We were worried about the gash in its leg, but decided that the saltwater would heal it. Together we carried the pelican to the water's edge.

The bird stood on one leg and then the other. It lifted its wings and tested them. Then all at once, it pushed off the beach and flew above the waves and out to sea.

With a great sense of satisfaction, Louise, the elderly man, and I smiled and applauded each other. Soon after, Louise and I climbed back in the water and continued our swim down the coastline. As we neared the finish of our fifteen-mile swim, near Santa Monica pier, a pelican splashed into the water nearby and paddled over to us. We looked closely and saw a gash in its leg. It was the same pelican.

The bird paddled with us to the pier, then left us to join a flock of pelicans flying north. We watched the birds glide magnificently above the breaking waves, riding the warm afternoon air currents until they were out of sight.

Two months later, Louise swam across the Catalina Channel in just over fifteen hours.

★

Lynne Cox has broken world records crossing the English Channel and swam the Bering Strait to promote peace and open the border between the U.S. and Russia. She has written for The New Yorker, Los Angeles Times Magazine, *and chronicled her life as an extreme athlete in* Swimming to Antarctica: Tales of a Long-Distance Swimmer. *She lives in Southern California.*

PAULA McDONALD

. * .

Waltz at the End of Earth

Amazing things happen when you journey
to the edge of the map.

THERE ARE MOMENTS WHEN A SUDDEN, UNEXPECTED CONNECtion is made somewhere in the world, powerful and undeniable. When the energy is exactly right, it doesn't seem to matter where you are. Things just happen as they should. My experience in a tiny hovel on a far-distant Chinese island was one of those moments.

Two of us were on our way to "End of Earth," the most remote beach on remote Hainan Island, the furthest south in a string of Chinese islands in the South China Sea. A ridiculous place to want to go; there's nothing there. But the ancient Chinese believed the earth ended at the southern tip of this largest of China's islands. Thus, to journey to "End of Earth" was to show great "strength and courage," qualities of utmost importance to the Chinese. To journey to "End of Earth" was to bring great good fortune to yourself. In such a strange way, my journey did.

Getting to Hainan Island from Guangzhou isn't easy. Eighteen-hour village-bus rides through the mountains with the inevitable breakdowns in the middle of the night are followed by tedious ferries, incomprehensible transfers, and more tedious ferries. To even attempt Hainan Island without speaking fluent Cantonese requires a strong belief in personal luck, guardian angels, and good fairies.

To this day, I can vividly remember every moment of that journey; for the life of me I can't figure out how we arranged it or what compelled us so completely at the time.

But, the journey itself is another tale. Suffice it to say that we found our way to "End of Earth" eventually, a peaceful, serene place with an aura of great continuity. Beyond, with quiet waves lapping at our feet, the sea seemed to stretch forever. Like the ancient Chinese, who could know what was out there? Or what would come next? What came next was one of the most important gifts of my life.

In a tiny village nearby, we stopped for lunch at a small roadside house, a hovel actually, one of those one-room shacks that serve as home, restaurant, and mini-zoo, a combination so common in rural China.

Joanne Turner, my fellow traveler, and I had eaten in many similar places in the few weeks since we'd met and completed a stint together as volunteers on a scientific project meant to catalog China's southern rainforests. We'd camped on remote mountain-tops, sea kayaked the uninhabited Outer Islands, trekked through leech-filled jungles, and eaten, standing up, in every street market in Southern China it seemed.

Along the way, we'd become expert pantomimists, ready smilers, and absolute gourmands on the street-food scene. The shabbiness of the shack didn't bother us. The luxury of eating from an actual table instead of a rock seemed rather civilized, in fact.

This particular shack was poor even by Chinese standards though. It held only the bare wooden table, a rope bed, and several cages full of eight- and ten-foot snakes. The dirt floor was swept clean, and an old bicycle hung on the wall. Nothing more adorned the place. Cooking, as is customary in the countryside, was done out back on an empty oil drum with a wood fire below.

The 80-year-old owner and her granddaughter immediately began to display their snakes. Out they came from their cages and were handed to us, one by one. Which did we want for lunch? We tried to pantomime that it was very hot, that we weren't very hungry after all, and that the snakes were very large. There would be so much waste.

Perhaps rabbit would be better, suggested our hosts. Or so we assumed as they took us to a shed in back where three rabbits were caged. Unable to look any bunny in the eye and then eat it, we politely tried to say that the rabbits were also too big. The only other choice seemed to be an old chicken pecking at the edge of the dirt lane, so we opted for him. Least of all possible sins, or so we thought.

Twenty minutes later, the food began arriving: the usual Chinese mystery soup, followed by several courses of vegetables, rice, and endless pots of steaming tea in the 100-degree heat. Finally the meat arrived.

It was unmistakably rabbit! Oh, lordy, where had we gone wrong? Perhaps we should have drawn pictures instead of doing charades. We ate it, of course. With grace and a good deal of hard swallowing. Not to would have caused a loss of face for the two gracious women whose humble hospitality we shared.

The heat was oppressive that day, as it is all over southern China in May, and even to sit still was to sit and drip. During lunch, the old woman kept smiling at me as if to say, "I forgive you for sweating in my house. There is no loss of face in this," and fanning me with a marvelously ingenious fan made completely of feathers. I had never seen anything like it.

Since there was literally nothing else in the one-room house, not even a change of clothes, and the fan seemed to be her only possession besides an old watch, I was careful not to admire it openly. Chinese custom demands the giving to guests of whatever they admire. But despite my intentional disregard of the fan, I was immensely grateful for the momentary illusion of coolness each whoosh brought.

Perhaps because I was trying so hard to ignore the feather fan, what happened next caught me completely by surprise.

Suddenly, for no apparent reason, the old woman broke into a great grin, hugged me hard, handed me the fan, and then hugged me again. I was stunned. It was obviously a gift, but her generosity, under the circumstances, was astonishing. What had prompted the act? What could I, a lanky, perspiring stranger with a sunburned nose, in her life for so short a time, have possibly done to deserve the gift of one of her few possessions? Nothing that I could conceive of, but something had changed dramatically in the little room. The old woman now sat smiling beatifically as though I had pleased her more than I could ever imagine. But I couldn't, for the life of me figure out how.

Despite the baking heat inside the house, we lingered awhile after lunch and drank more tea just to stay and not seem to rush away. And then, to our amazement, when her granddaughter finally left to take care of other chores, the old woman began to speak in halting English, obviously a language she had not used for decades. Bit by bit, straining to understand the stumbling words, we learned her story.

Her husband had been imprisoned under Mao for being a follower of Chiang Kai-Shek and had died a prisoner. She had watched as he led away. She never saw him again.

Before the Cultural Revolution the woman had been a teacher, the daughter of educated diplomats, one of the new regime's despised intellectuals. After the Communist victory in China, she had been exiled from Shanghai to the remote island village for the double sins of being educated and being the wife of a political enemy. She had lived in the isolated village for more than 30 years, surviving as best she could by cooking and selling the snakes and rabbits she and her granddaughter were able to trap.

Her story, told with no rancor, captured our hearts, and despite the need to get on, we stayed. The long-forgotten English words seemed to get easier for her as we asked questions about her life and encouraged her to reminisce. She told us of her childhood, of traveling and learning English at embassies as a youngster. Memories of another, so very different life. Yet, for all her losses, she truly seemed to have no bitterness. With one strange exception. When I asked her directly if she had regrets, she could think of only one: that she had never learned to waltz.

One of her most vivid childhood memories was of being taken, as a young girl, to a grand ball in Hong Kong where there were many English guests in attendance. The music was international that night, the first time she had heard anything besides the harsh, sharp cacophony of China's music, and suddenly the ballroom was filled with swirling skirts and the sweetest sounds she had ever heard. Couples were waltzing, and, to the young Chinese girl, it was the most beautiful sight in the world. Someday she would grow up to become one of those graceful waltzing women.

She grew up, but China changed. There were no more waltzes. And now there were no more illusions in her life.

In the silence that followed the story, I took her hand across the table. Then I quietly asked if she would still like to learn to waltz. Here. Now.

The slow smile that spread across her face was my answer. We stood and moved together toward our ballroom floor, an open space of five feet of hard-packed dirt between the table and the bed. "Please, God," I prayed, "let me remember a waltz. Any waltz. And let me remember how to lead."

We started shakily, me humming Strauss, stepping on her toes. But soon we got smoother, bolder, louder. "The Blue Danube" swelled and filled the room. Her baggy Mao pajama pants became a swirling skirt, she became young and beautiful again, and I became a handsome foreigner, tall, sure, strong…perhaps a prince who carried her away. Away from her destiny at "End of Earth."

The feather fan hangs on my office wall today, next to her picture. Next to our picture. The two of us, hands clasped, smiling strangers from such different worlds, waltzing around a steaming hut in a forsaken spot I visited by chance that day. That day I met strength and courage at "End of Earth."

✳

Paula McDonald lives on the beach in Rosarito, Mexico. On the clearest of days, if she squints, she can almost see China's "End of Earth." When the waves are quiet, she can certainly hear Strauss.

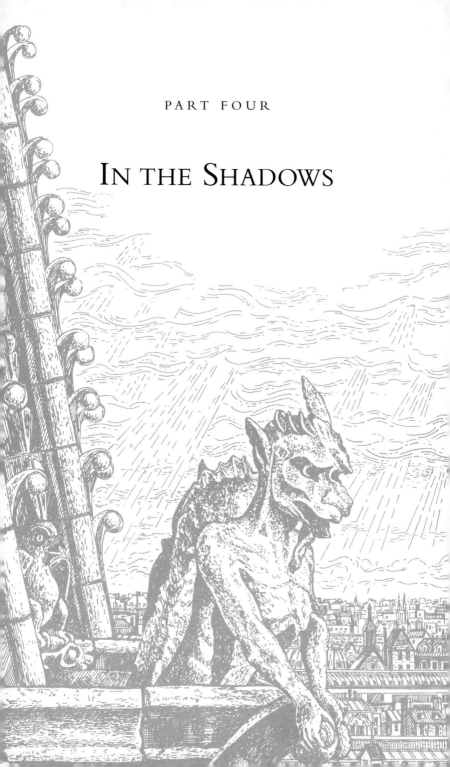

PART FOUR

IN THE SHADOWS

MARCEL F. LAVENTURIER

Destination Paris

A young man meets his destiny.

BEFORE REACHING PARIS, I ESCAPED FROM ST-QUENTIN.

The town of St-Quentin, the capital of Picardie in northern France.

The year was 1940. The German army had invaded Holland, Belgium, Luxembourg, and France. The only remaining obstacle to Hitler's total domination of Western Europe was Great Britain, a few tantalizing miles across the Channel. In the fall, the German High Command implemented the first phase of Operation Sea Lion: saturation bombing of the British seaports and the London Blitz. South of the Belgian border, north of Paris, the invasion force was readying an attack for the spring of 1941.

At the time, I was nineteen, an American student living with an uncle in Belgium. The German authorities in our small town had paid scant attention to me until September 10 when it was announced that President Roosevelt had transferred 50 American destroyers to the Royal Navy. The local commandant considered this an overt act of war for which he held me personally responsible. I was ordered to report to the Kreiskommandatur in Brussels to justify my status as a non-combatant neutral alien. There was a complication—I carried a valid American passport and was U.S. born, but the fact that both my mother and father had been born in France made me a French citizen according to French and German laws. My other problem was that I had failed to report for conscription in the French army when I reached eighteen; this made me a deserter as well. Rather than report to the Germans to face jail or deportation, I joined the Belgian Underground.

My best friend was the leader of a small group of resisters who helped escaped allied prisoners evade the Gestapo. He controlled black market and smuggling rings which he used to finance his clandestine operations. He signed me on as a courier. For a couple of months I lived in safe houses and smuggled uncut diamonds from Antwerp across the border into France; occasionally, I served as an English interpreter. That November, the Germans changed the currency laws for the occupied countries, and our group was able to steal one million newly printed Occupation Reichmarks. The money had to be spread around to our operatives in a way that it could not be traced. As my final job for the Underground, I was given the opportunity to earn my passage back to the U.S. by smuggling part of the loot to our safe house in Paris. Up to that time the border was fairly porous, our couriers carrying false papers moved people and money back and forth regularly. What we didn't realize was that this red zone, as it came to be known, had been placed on high alert by the Germans to prevent spying on the troop movements. Special passes from the Kreiskommandatur in Brussels were required for civilian travel. All I had was my American passport. To hide my share of the swag, 150,000 Reichmarks, I divided the bills into two bundles which I wrapped in brown paper then baked in two large loaves of peasant bread. Bread was rationed and I would not attract attention by carrying some in my luggage. When I boarded the Brussels–Paris express, I carefully selected a seat in a second class compartment closest to an exit.

The train had been chugging along for some time through the wintry countryside when it slowed down and finally stopped. I stepped out of the compartment and saw two German military policemen wearing the insignia of the "Feldengendarmerie" enter at the opposite end of the carriage. As the train started slowly, I reached for the handle on the exit door, ready to jump, but there were sentries posted every few feet along the track. The door to the rest room was at my back, I opened it and locked myself in, trapped like an animal. In a cold sweat with my pulse racing, I prayed that the police would overlook my hiding place. Soon, I heard a rap on the door. I didn't respond at first but when it persisted, louder and louder, I opened the door and two of the largest German soldiers that I had ever seen walked in; one stood in front and one in back of me.

"*Papiers?*"

I showed them my passport, they compared me to my photo then the largest one said, "*Zu schen sein passierschein?*"

"*Nicht verstehen,*" I answered.

He smiled, "*Mitkommen.*"

They frisked me for weapons and took me back to my seat where one of them guarded me until we reached the next stop— St-Quentin. A six-man squad of soldiers waited on the platform. The policeman handed my passport to a corporal; three other prisoners joined us, then we were marched double file across the tracks, over a bridge, then right in the center of the street going uptown. Curious civilians stopped to stare at us, traffic went around us. Soon, we stopped at a building over which flew a huge swastika flag. The troopers herded us into a room filled with frightened men and women; some were crying. They didn't make room for me so I sat on my fancy yellow leather suitcase. The corporal of the guard handed our papers to two Gestapo men who sat at the opposite end of the room. One of them came to me, motioned me off my suitcase and took it away. The smell of my terror was added to that of the other prisoners. A Gestapo seated at the table piled high with papers pointed and shouted questions at us in German. An interpreter translated his questions. I understood most of what the Gestapo was saying, but when my turn came, he pointed at me and shouted, "*Sprechen Sie Deutsch?*"

I looked blankly at him and kept silent.

The translator said, "Do you understand German?"

"Unfortunately, no. Only English and French."

My answer sent the Gestapo into a rage, he got red in the face, started shouting louder and banging his fist on the table. He threw some papers in a folder but kept on raving and making menacing gestures.

The translator said, "He is turning you over to the judge for immediate sentencing. He says that you are a Frenchman with a fake American passport sent here to spy for the British. If it was up to him, he'd call out the firing squad and shoot you without a trial, this minute."

The other prisoners moved away from me as if I were a leper. I began to perspire, my hands shook and my mouth and throat went dry. One of the Gestapo soldiers pushed me into the next room, past the raving maniac who was still screaming.

It served as a court room. On an elevated dais a small bald-headed, sour-faced man dressed in a black uniform sat at a large desk. He picked through my papers, looked at me with disgust and speaking in French said, "This court is tired of adjudicating cases that are not in our jurisdiction. You will be tried in a military court in Brussels. You are remanded back to Belgium."

In German, he ordered the Gestapo to take me away and to ship me back on the next train.

I was taken to a small room where three French *gendarmes* sat at a small table playing cards. The guard propelled me towards them and in an accented French told them to push me across the red line as soon as possible. They interrupted their card game and looked at me with professional interest, trying to place me in some criminal category. What was this well-dressed young man up to?

One of them, not unkindly said, "Sit down and relax. It will take some time for the Germans to fill out all their forms. They love paper work. There isn't a train north until tomorrow anyway. You will sleep in our jail tonight."

Ever since my arrest I had lived in a state of disorganized terror as if I'd been thrown overboard in a vast ocean full of man-eaters. I was desperately paddling to stay afloat while dozens of other prisoners were clinging to the sides of a boat. They were torn away, one by one, by the attacking sharks. Sitting in the boat, which flew the swastika, drunken soldiers amused themselves, pushing men, women and children over the side. I was living a nightmare.

The benign attitude of the French *gendarmes* reassured me. It changed my outlook from terror to simple fear. It is astonishing what a kind word can accomplish in a desperate situation. The *gendarmes* ignored me and returned to their noisy game. In about an hour, a German brought my suitcase and handed the policemen a manila envelope. I asked the sergeant if I could get some cigarettes out of my bag. He nodded yes. I opened it. I could tell that it had been searched, but both loaves of bread appeared intact. My spirits soared from despair to hope. Everything was not lost. My luck was changing; with courage, imagination, and determination, I might escape the sharks. When the card game ended, the *gendarmes* added their score, exchanged money and then turned towards me. I offered them cigarettes and asked them if it was possible for us to stop and buy some food on our way to the jail.

"If you have money to pay for it, we'll gladly take you to a restaurant."

"If it's OK, I would gladly buy drinks and dinner all around."

They looked at each other, but they didn't answer. One of them escorted me out, through a back door, down an alley to a closed restaurant. We entered through the kitchen. It was empty except for the owners. We were finishing our first drink when the other two *gendarmes* showed up. I called for more drinks. We enjoyed a five course dinner with bottles of expensive wine with each course; then cognac and more wine. I told them that I was an American student trying to reach Paris prior to returning home. My arrest was a total mistake. I am sure that they didn't believe me. We played cards and drank until midnight. Naturally, I lost heavily. Since it was past curfew, the jail was closed and I was such a grand fellow and model prisoner, they decided that I should take a room upstairs; drunk as I was they said that they were certain that I wouldn't try to escape. Afterwards, hugged by the comfort and warmth of a feather bed, I decided that the odds were so poor that I could run away in the middle of the night, without papers, in a strange town crawling with Germans, that I planned to wait until daybreak before making my move. I fell asleep and dreamt of Paris.

Next morning, shaved and dressed in my tweeds, I was ready to step out onto the wet pavement when one of the *gendarmes* showed up. He seemed surprised that I was still around. They must have really thought that I was a spy. Mustering all my courage, I asked him if he carried a gun. No, the Germans didn't trust him, he was armed with a night stick and a whistle. If a prisoner tried to run away, his orders were to try to restrain him and to blow his whistle to alert the German and French police to come to his aid. Outside, the rain had stopped but had been replaced by a cold gray fog, the kind that chills you right through to the bone marrow. I took an envelope filled with currency and put it in his hand.

"I'd appreciate it if you could give me my passport and wait a couple of hours before blowing your whistle."

He put the envelope in his tunic pocket, handed me my passport out of the manila folder, opened the door, pointed down the hill towards the railroad station.

"That is the way south. Keep off the paved roads, try the fields. If you get caught tell them that you knocked me down and overpowered me. Good luck."

The streets were deserted, I walked across the Marne canal without seeing anyone. When I reached the railroad tracks, I entered the plowed fields slippery with brown clay. The fog was thicker around the waterways and the going so tough that I doubted that any patrols would venture into the countryside that morning. I stumbled along keeping the barely visible railroad lines to my right. From time to time, I stopped to rest and to listen to the sounds around me. I heard voices, dog barks, train, car and wagon noises. I was floating in a sea of fog with everything near but out of sight. Once, I was stopped by a canal. I didn't panic, I backtracked alongside it and crossed the water at a railroad bridge which was left unguarded. Around noon, the fog eased a little. I had reached the outskirts of a small city. It was the town of Tergniers, a rail center with squat houses huddled around the station. Since leaving St-Quentin I hadn't been challenged by anyone, my luck was holding. Before entering the town, I sat down and changed to a clean pair of shoes from my suitcase. I left my muddy ones in a culvert and, nonchalantly carrying my suitcase, I walked into the station. The platform was full of German soldiers. When a train with a Paris destination ground to a noisy stop, everyone including me jumped on board.

Struggling with my suitcase, I walked through the first class section until I located a compartment with an empty seat. All other seats were occupied by young officers. They helped me heave my coat and my bag onto the rack. They spoke to me, I answered "*Guten tag. Jawohl....*" and smiled a lot. I intimated that I was Flemish, "*Flemmisch Sprechen. Deutsch verstehen.*"

Looking around, I noticed that all the signs in the car were in German. God. In my haste, I had jumped on a troop train which had originated in the Fatherland. My traveling companions mistook me for one of their civilian surrogates—a collaborator. They couldn't have treated me nicer; having exhausted most of my vocabulary and before I could arouse any suspicion, I had to find a way out—not the toilet this time. A steward playing a glockenspiel stuck his head in the compartment and announced the second seating for lunch. I followed him to an ornate dining car. He thrust a reservation book at me to sign in. I wrote something illegible followed by the street address of a hotel in Antwerp. He waved me to a small table for two; except for some ladies, I noticed that I was the only civilian there. I tried to make myself as inconspicuous as possible by looking out the window. The sun had finally broken through the mist. At a large table opposite mine, four German officers in full dress, their tunics covered with iron crosses, ribbons and medals were lingering over their desserts and plotting the train's itinerary on a map. They observed the countryside with binoculars and talked about having traveled through there before. I overheard them say respectfully "General." When the train reached Compiègne, the place where the armistices in 1918 and 1940 had been signed, they laughed and called for champagne. The General stood and proposed a toast. Everyone in the dining salon stood, including me. He noticed that I was raising my water glass so he directed the steward to bring me some champagne. On command, we toasted Germany's victorious armies. As the only person not in uniform, I realized that I stood out like a sore thumb and expected the worst. Should the General try to talk to me, I was finished. When he stood up to leave, he directed the waiter to bring me two half-filled bottles of white wine and some cake from his table. I stood up, bowed and said, "*Danke schön, Herr General.*"

He gave me the Nazi salute, "Heil Hitler."

I responded in kind. When I sat down, I was pleased with my performance. My Heil Hitler to the General certainly impressed the rest of the diners who cast furtive glances in my direction. I really must be important for the General to take notice of me. The waiter brought the menu and I ordered sausage and red cabbage in my most guttural Flemish. The dining room was full and there were some officers waiting to be seated but because of my short acquaintance with my host I was allowed to savor their best Rhine wines and eat their gourmet food at my leisure like a privileged member of the Master Race. Had I been dressed in shabby clothes, worn muddy shoes and sporting a two day's growth of beard, I would be traveling on a train going in the opposite direction to a certain death. Clothes make the man; this morning I was haggling with a French policeman for my freedom and now I was dining in the German senior officers' salon. My long walk and the dangers I had faced sharpened my appetite; I did justice to the meal and the chocolate cake, the first chocolate that I had tasted in months. The waiter brought a box of cigars and a brandy snifter. He opened the box and I selected one as he poured me a half glass of Courvoisier from the General's bottle. When I reached for a lighter, he gave me a light and I lit the cigar like an expert. I gave him a couple of hundred francs for his trouble. For my taste I find Courvoisier a little sweet—not enough oak. I prefer a more robust Cognac, but this being wartime and given the circumstances I must learn to make do.... The cigar was Dutch Sumatra perfect, it built a wonderful cone of ashes. The train rattled through the last miles of our journey. I smiled with contentment and a young lady two tables away smiled back. I hadn't meant to smile at her, it was a reaction to my change of fortune; happiness like misery is easily transmitted. I was jettisoning my anguish every mile that I traveled away from St-Quentin and towards Paris. Here I was in the midst of my enemies, enjoying their hospitality while in my bag I carried 150,000 stolen marks. I went from the depth of despair to the heights of elation. Paris was not only my destination, it was my destiny. When we reached the drab industrial approaches to the city, the train slowed and I decided that it was safe for me to return to my seat. The rail lines around the Gare du Nord were guarded by anti-aircraft batteries. When the train stopped, all the military personnel were allowed on the platform. When I tried to exit, my passage was blocked by military policemen. I looked out the window and saw the reason why. The huge glass and steel building was festooned with swastikas. An honor guard stood at attention facing the train. A band played "*Deutschland Über Alles.*" The General and his staff reviewed the troops, saluted them, then the honor guard changed formation, and the band attacked a lively march tune as they goose-stepped out of the station. The General and all the troops followed, then me, whistling and marching in step, carrying my precious yellow leather suitcase towards freedom and the Paris boulevards.

I soon learned that the General who unwittingly helped me achieve the first stage of my escape was the new military governor of Paris.

*

Marcel Laventurier was born in the United States but spent his youth in Belgium and France. After escaping from the Nazis he served in the US Navy throughout World War II, married in 1945, and became a pharmacist in California. This story is one of a series that he has written about his wartime experiences.

RAJENDRA S. KHADKA

* * *

Sharing the Pain

A sometime voyeur searches
for creatures of the night.

As the Hindus and Buddhists know only too well, in the
beginning was Desire, rather than the Word, as the Christians
would say. Having heard whisperings about a dark and mysterious
sado-masochistic-bondage *Scene* in San Francisco, and being a good
Hindu, I acted upon my whimsical desire and made my way to a
sado-parlor of some renown.

The bouncer/gate boy, pale white but in black leather, motorcycle garb, a fuzz of vertical hair running from the lower lip to the
chin, is from Alabama. Guarding the entrance to the sado parlor is
his full-time job. He is affable and chatty, and is occasionally joined
by an SP (sado parlor) gal, all hugs and girlish giggles as she mingles and mushes with the bouncer boy. Intricate, colorful tattoos
are visible wherever her flesh shows; a sparkling metallic loop
pierces her belly-button; more metal loops between her nostrils
and drips below her nose, the kind of nose ring one sees among the
cattle of India and Nepal. They are both young and hip, on the
cutting edge, if not in the "pierced zone." The bouncer boy sounds
uncharacteristically optimistic and bourgeois. Says he, "My father,
back home, he approves! I have a steady job, a car, and a motorcycle.
I'm looking into going to college soon." No nihilism here, for sure.

"When does the club close?" I ask.

"Three in the morning, but most start leaving around one-thirty, last call. So the less intelligent ones drift off to other bars where they can drink. The club has really been supported by rockers and others who like to come here and hang out after hours."

I like the way he said, "The less intelligent ones." The boy will go far, I know.

Another black leathered male joins him. He has a braided goatee. The bouncer boy laughs wildly. Stroking his thin, vertical, faux goatee, he gloats, "Man, I almost braided my goatee too, but I'm really glad I didn't. I shaved it off. Most of it."

The gal with the cattle nose ring now throws herself into the arms of the newcomer with the braided goatee. Hugs and mushes make me think there is more "touchy feely" here than rage and despair.

Inside, I pay a five dollar entry fee. The back of my wrist is stamped so I have "in-out privileges." Loud, thumping, lyricless industrial music reverberates throughout the cavernous space. Some clean-cut college kids wearing jeans and button-down shirts are playing pool and drinking bottled beer, swaggering as only college kids can do. The bar, the cavernous dance floor, the entire club is almost empty. Above the dance floor hang slowly revolving "disco balls" the likes of which I haven't seen since my own undergraduate days when the crowd would go wild when some sort of mist rose from the dance floor. Looks as if things haven't changed much in two decades.

Next to the entrance, opposite the pool tables, two chic underdressed young girls in stockings, very short skirts, hair streaked in henna, rings and bracelets all over fingers and wrists, high heels, are selling rings, playing cards that have anti-drugs and anti-smoking messages (is there irony in these messages, I wonder? humor macabre?), and t-shirts with logos of "Bondage a Go Go" around a picture of a bound woman—fifteen bucks, thank you.

I go upstairs to another bar where a woman who appears to be of mixed race—a blonde black woman—is selling more stuff: incense, candles, massage oils in tiny bottles, colorful salt crystals in plastic bags, fragrant bubble bath items. I'm beginning to feel that the club is a meeting ground of the new-agers and the leather-clad, tattooed, body-parts-pierced "rough crowd," with both displaying the aggressive spirit of fin-de-siecle capitalism.

I order a beer. No one is handcuffed to the bar. I ask the bartender about it and he says that that specific bondage item has been taken off the menu. Diagonally across the bar, there is a corral where a few young men and women mill about, the main attraction, as it turned out. The girls look suspiciously under-age, precocious even as they look tough, very under-dressed, all black clothing that stretches when even a muscle (or in most cases, fat) moves. A girl with long, thick, puffy hair has a black t-shirt on that says on the front "Fuck Me" and on the back "Then Leave." Some whips with stripped leather are on display on the wall above a sign that says, "Toys 4 Sale." There it is again, this optimistic spirit of the entrepreneur in this cavern of delinquency.

Food is also available, and near the kitchen, a notice of health again: "No smoking near the kitchen area and condiments."

Meanwhile, the patrons are arriving. It's a mixed crowd: college kids, 9–5 working folks, Generation X-ers. Dress ranges from t-shirts and jeans to bondage gear. Lots of silver jewelry and tattoos on much exposed flesh. There are many bondage wanna-bes, especially pre-pubescent suburban girls, many wearing slips and bra, and a coat to throw over when they step out to catch some fresh air, for the air is getting thick as the bodies begin to arrive and the action on the dance floor and in the corral begins in earnest.

I meet a couple who tell me their names are Daphne and Master Dick. Daphne is a young woman dressed all in black; Dick is thin-lipped, hooded-eyed, and apparently twice her age. She is getting an "electric" caress by a short, tubby, sweaty but very pleasant man who has some sort of a drill-like instrument, wired and connected to a socket and from which bluish sparks fly. He runs his nails all over her, her fishnet, crotchless stockings, black vinyl skirt, false eyelashes, magenta-black lipstick and eye-shades, black nails, but *false* nose ring, just as Master Dick has a *false* ear ring. One can tell these are not serious disciples of the diabolical Marquis de Sade, may the Devil torture his soul. This false note is especially jarring when one sees women stick out their pierced tongues!

Daphne shudders and sometimes squeals as the sweaty, tubby electric caresser runs his nails over her bare arms and runs his tongue over that exposed flesh. He moves his hands in and around the fish-netted legs, as Master Dick glares. Daphne shudders with delight. The Hindu licks his suddenly dry lips.

Soon, there are butts upturned on a carpenter's horse. Fat butts, skinny butts, bikinied butts, tattooed butts: they are stroked, swished, smacked. Girls' arms are spread and clamped to an over-hanging bar; they're blindfolded with a fancy accessory that looks like aviator sunglasses. Then they are stroked with feathers, furs, whips, tassels; a lone woman—hands bound—is kissed, stroked, licked, and tantalized by a half-dozen men and women. The bound woman squirms.

On a sawhorse, a small, thin young woman is bound upturned, her naked upper body exposed; she is only wearing a leather bikini bottom. Her Master (Pleasure-Giver) works on her like a dedicated artist, using a shining hunter's knife (no doubt dull-edged) and a small, curved scythe where the sharpened blade shines like a crescent moon. The master is using both knives all over her body. The girl has her eyes closed. Her high-heeled feet tremble occasionally. Her lips, like the Hovering Hindu's, are dry. She doesn't lick them, unlike the Hindu.

I overhear a thick frat boy say in bewildered joy, "You mean these dudes get paid to whip those chicks?"

Two suburban post-pubescent gals, blonde and brave, stand behind me watching the master do his thing with the knives. One says to the other, "The first drop of blood and I'm out the friggin' door."

And so the action continues. The dance floor is full of swaying, whirling bodies; blue, red, green spotlights dance off the revolving disco ball above the dance floor, which is thick with cigarette and incense smoke, as well as body heat. Yet it is all paradoxically unerotic. The body does not respond, the soul remains sacred. Even the voyeur is quickly bored. It is quickly becoming comical. The participants in their S&M acts are young and eager, and drinking from bottles of "Jolt" cola, as if more adrenaline were required to launch their eager bodies and souls.

And as the Hovering Hindu shuffles around, he is thinking of Dostoevsky's *Notes from the Underground,* and he thinks that only a person with a Dostoevskian delirium, with his epileptic seizure, could do an extended riff on the scene around me. But then maybe not. For this rather tame, wanna-be scene lacks even that "fear and loathing" that might attract the latter-day disciple of gonzo journalist Hunter Thompson.

I think of Dostoevsky because he speaks about how when a person is jaded by normal, ordinary pleasure, he seeks to go beyond these normal bounds because the normal is boring. So the Russian writer remembers some historical Queen who had golden needles stuck into the breasts of her slave girls, and got pleasure from watching their pain.

At two a.m., his mind full of tattoos, black leather, silver jewelry, butts, boobs, pubes, and Dostoevsky, the Hovering Hindu decides it is time to return to his hovel. For there he will find peace, and for him, that is bondage enough.

★

Rajendra S. Khadka was born in Nepal and educated by Jesuits in Kathmandu and Yankees in New England. His desultory career pursuits have included freelance journalism, managing a movie theater during the pre-VCR days, and a chef-on-call. He is the editor of Travelers' Tales Nepal *and currently lives in Atlanta where his wife is pursuing a doctorate in education.*

Heavenly Wardrobe

Put it on for eternity.

I HAD PRETTY MUCH RUN THROUGH THE OPTIONS OF FORTUNE telling for the living but I was interested in one more thing: influencing the afterlife. I'd always wanted to see the paper offerings that Chinese burn at services for the dead to insure that certain possessions of the good life are taken with them into heaven. Some Chinese even have the real thing burned. A college student I'd met on my last trip to Hong Kong told me her grandfather had exacted a promise that his beloved fur coat would be burned at his funeral.

Most people settle for paper effigies, whether of things they own or would like to own. A friend patiently led me to the neighborhood where the paper offerings shops were located, on Queen's Road West. I expected something ethereal, but these stores looked as practical inside as a Midwestern dry cleaners. In one an older man and his daughter sat on stools eating noodles from cups, regarding us without speaking. We peered at shelves full of boxes of six gold foil watches each, fat wads of fake money, written on the Bank of Hell, and then looked up at the ceiling where three-foot long paper mâché servants dangled. The shop seemed empty, but Betty explained that most families special-ordered items for the deceased—cars, furniture, airplanes—so there was not a lot of stock

to see. We did see one shocking pink villa, like a junior high student's diorama, complete with Mercedes Benz in the driveway, servants, mistresses, and tiny trays of food.

I bought some watches and money, but decided I could never get one of the yard-long servants into my luggage. As we left, we paused under the overhang just outside the shop. Hanging from the beams were gaily wrapped packages with ribbons and dragon stickers. I asked Betty what they were.

"Clothes for the next life."

The packages looked about the size of a good wool sweater wrapped as a Christmas present. The bundles came in two colors, red or green. One for women, the other for men. I asked what the clothes looked like, but Betty didn't know. "We never open them. It isn't done. We just burn them at the funeral still wrapped," she said, her serious eyes steady.

"But suppose it's just shredded paper? How do you know?"

"We don't," she said quietly. "I guess it could be. We just don't open them."

I ducked back in the shop and bought a package of the women's variety.

The heat and humidity kept the city under its grip that entire week. We distracted ourselves by eating too much of too many delicious things: fried prawn balls in chili sauce, sticky rice balls with black sesame in sweet wine sauce, pigeon, abalone, sea cucumber, and drunken chicken. In between we shopped, buying hand-worked pillows, beaded handbags, leather slippers, jade children's amulets, and silk bomber jackets. Normally, I try not to eat too much or buy too much while traveling, but in Hong Kong all bets are off.

The next time I remember being really cool again was just after stepping into the plane bound for home. I mopped my brow with the icy cloth offered by the stewardess, sank into the seat and went to sleep.

At home, I tossed the package of clothes for the hereafter on the bedroom bureau. No matter how many times my eye rested on it in the weeks that followed, I didn't open it. I have always had a horror of being disappointed, in both small and large matters. I was curious about the clothes, but not curious enough to face there being only a wad of shredded paper, like a mass of convoluted cookie fortunes.

The days were getting shorter and slightly cooler on the farm where I live when late one night, near midnight, the phone rang in the bedroom.

It was my friend Pat's sister, calling from another city, where Pat was in the hospital. "You'd better come now, right away, if you want to see her one more time and say good-bye," Karen said quickly.

I hung up and sat on the bed, my mind racing. While I'd known she was failing, I hadn't realized Pat was that close to the end. While I'd been in Hong Kong she was still traveling for work, at a meeting in Chicago. I called the airline and started tossing things in my suitcase for an early morning flight. At the last minute my eye was caught by the light from the bedside lamp shining on the package from Hong Kong. I threw it in.

When I got there, Pat was still aware, and although very thin, her eyes were still their incredible electric blue and her cheerful, energetic self shone out even in this condition. She knew time was running out and she wanted to get everything done.

Surprising us all, she did not die that day, or the next, but lived for almost two more weeks. Every night in her hospital room, her friends and family, with Pat's direction, arranged for entertainment of some kind. One night everyone shared photos of vacations we had taken together. Another evening a music professor came and played classical guitar selections so Pat could choose the music she wanted at her memorial service. Her grandchildren came and shared drawings from school. A sonogram of the grandson she would never meet was tacked to the bulletin board.

One evening I brought out the bright green package from Hong Kong, (for Chinese, green is the color of eternity) and asked Pat if she would like to open it and take the clothes into the here-after. "Oh great, sure!" She smiled her good broad smile, ready for anything and still positive about any new idea.

At 7:30 p.m. we all gathered around her bed as she pulled the red ribbons from the soft package. "Did you like Hong Kong?" she asked, still hungry for new information. I started to tell her about the way it looks silver and green, with sleek metallic buildings backed by the lush undulating hills of the New Territories; about the shops selling snake and "1,000-year-old eggs"; about the sweet-sour smell that is Hong Kong, made up of delicious street food cooking, gas fumes, fish, and expensive perfume.

But just then the package fell open, revealing the most beautiful heavy paper evening pajamas, with delicate embossed gold leaves. Frogs made the closures. As Pat picked them up, delighted, a paper undershirt, a flowered fan, and a paper cape also fell out. In the cen-ter, revealed last, were a pair of three-dimensional black Chinese slippers, of paper mâché.

The group around the bed sighed its wonder in unison, as we lay the outfit out on Pat, who looked down and smoothed them out on herself carefully, just as she had always done with real clothes, meticulous as ever.

"Gee, they're beautiful, I'll be the best dressed one there," she said, with her old, true laugh.

I thought then about how unpredictable life is. About Mr. Tsui, the Hong Kong fortune teller who said not to worry, to take everything step by step, and not to be selfish. Maybe life is not pre-dictable, but maybe it is manageable, with good friends, the right advice, and a little luck.

✳

Judith Babcock Wylie is a travel writer, editor, newspaper columnist, and writing instructor who has been writing travel stories and essays full-time for twenty years. Her work has appeared in such publications as Travel & Leisure, The London Financial Times, Modern Maturity, San Francisco Chronicle, *and* Los Angeles Times. *She is the author of* Best Places Destinations Central California Coast *and the editor of* Travelers' Tales Love & Romance. *She lives on an organic apple farm in Santa Cruz, California and writes in a rebuilt cabin overlooking the ocean.*

Wild Trek Dog

*Cultures can clash over a
dog's role in society.*

IT WAS MY THIRD SEASON AS A TREK LEADER IN THE ATLAS Mountains of Morocco, working alongside the Berber tribespeople of the region. Accompanying tourists from all over the world on treks in these high desert mountains, I was solely responsible for all aspects of the expedition. It was a very demanding job, especially for a woman in an Islamic culture, and could be quite lonely, among the constant changeover of people.

We were passing through a valley that was rarely frequented by tourists. The villages clinging to the rugged mountainsides in the searing heat were extremely poor, the houses made of mud and woven cedar boughs. Our evening destination was a tented camp on terraces above the river in a gorge below. On our approach, inevitably, a screaming torrent of children would gush towards us, plastic shoes flapping, arms flailing, so curious to see *"les Anglais"* and beg for rich foreign sweets. They were filthy and smelt of animal dung and urine, but were so wonderfully vital and strong, and quite exceptionally beautiful. The Berbers are originally a Caucasian race who inhabited these mountains before the Arab invasion following the birth of Islam. They have intermarried and absorbed the Islamic religion, but still maintain a distinctly different cultural identity. Their exclusive gene pool can be seen in the blue and green eyes and red and blond hair that catches your eye among the creamy-dark skins. The people are fine-featured and have an elegance of carriage that defies the back-breaking toil of their subsistence lifestyle. The children have rosy cheeks over fine bones, bright white smiles, and a shyness that makes them utterly enchanting.

In Islamic culture, dogs are unclean. This means they have no status and should not be touched. The historical provenance of this notion is understandable. Wild and stray dogs in hot countries carry disease and parasites dangerous to man. They prey on small livestock, are generally unkempt and aggressive, feed on human waste, and have a "sly" or devious nature, the tenacious cunning essential to their survival. In an environment where man competes with the elements of both desert and mountain to live, animals are viewed only in terms of their usefulness. A dog's utility is in providing warning by barking at strangers, or herding goats and sheep.

To Westerners, the treatment of animals in Islam may seem harsh and barbaric. My experience of living closely with these ancient tribespeople persuades me that a ruthlessly hard lifestyle dictates maximum use of all resources, including animals. It was only 60 years ago that recurrent rape and pillage, massive infant mortality, hacking at each other with sabers, cutting off limbs as punishment and piling the heads of enemies at town gates, occurred as normal. When people themselves live in circumstances we'd wish to rescue animals from, then kindness to animals is a luxurious concept a poor Muslim can't be expected to understand.

Most Berbers do not hurt their animals purposefully. It is forbidden in the Koran. Livestock suffers harsh treatment and is kept for food or work. But the children, despite angelic faces and bubbling laughter, can be unutterably cruel.

My first awareness of Tizi was of a tiny, golden, furry bundle suspended in mid-air between two ragged boys. A six-week-old puppy, little floppy ears, slightly paler than her corn-gold puppy fur, and an almost white baby muzzle with the faintest freckles. She was squealing a rather angry yowl, and gnawing at the thumb

pinching one foreleg. It was only when her tone changed to a cur-
dling scream that she swung from peripheral vision to the focus of
my attention as I realized the boys intended something awful. They
were pulling her apart, one foreleg each, back legs kicking her
agony into the air. The boys were young, not more than five or six
years old, and laughing; enjoying the frenzied reaction they were
getting from hurting this pretty creature.

"Hey!" I shouted, furious, striding over and gripping one boy's
arm. I rattled off in French, pushing the boys apart. They giggled,
enjoying my frenzied reaction even more than the dog's. I grabbed
the puppy, who was limp, in what I was to discover was the safest
"unresponsive" pose a helpless puppy could assume in the face of
such terrible treatment. Children clustered round, all trying to grab
the dog. I held her high in one hand and gruffly shouted and
pushed them off. Suddenly, this puppy was a valuable commodity.
A Westerner had taken an interest. I realized that, now she was a
sensation, her fate in the village would be desperate. She would be
fought over because I had interfered, and would probably suffer a
brutal death.

Deciding what to do was complicated. Because she was a female
and would produce more unwanted whelps, she was destined to
find an early death anyway, either by torture or starvation. Only
male dogs were kept for guarding or herding. Also, I was emotionally involved. I had just returned from Alaska, where I had spent a
winter alone, living a wilderness lifestyle with a husky dog team for
freighting and transporting. I had come to be totally dependent on
the dogs, not just for hauling wood and water, but for companion-
ship, comedy, interest, and a binding friendship. I was very ready
for a canine companion, and what better life for a dog than roaming the mule-trails of the high Atlas! I decided simply: she had no
future without us.

I knew, within a few seconds of rescuing her, that this was a huge
personal responsibility for me, and that her life beyond the summer
season was now my burden. I would grow fond of this dog but ultimately have to leave her. However, the immediate circumstances
dictated unequivocally that we take her with us, at least out of the

village. I kidded myself that we could search for a home for her enroute. I was already smitten by her over-size paws, speckled chocolate eyes, and uncoordinated but enthusiastic energy. So, I arrived at camp with new puppy in tow. She had snuggled into me as I carried her, but remained limp over my arm. It seemed to me that this pup had learned from her short and tough life so far that it was futile to try to defy humankind.

The clients were unaware of any incident when I arrived with this mixture of adorable puppy and parasitic filth. Reactions were mixed. A few were immediately in love, others were disgusted that I could bring fleas so near to their tents. Of course, I could only keep her with their permission. Some were not at all keen. The priorities were to feed her; I was surprised how thin and bony she was beneath the fur, and then to wash her. She was *filthy* and lousy.

The puppy devoured plate after plate of meat and bread. The Berber muleteers were fascinated by my attention to her and concern for her health. Within half an hour the entire group was gathered around this fluffy bundle that was rolling and pouncing, now with enormous engorged stomach, with purr-like growls, and gnawing at everything with pin-like teeth. The puppy had won them over! She was coming with us.

Everyone's first preoccupation was a name. English doggy names abounded, but soon it was unanimous that we choose a Moroccan name. The Berbers were consulted and we had a wonderful evening around the fire, both cultures sharing ideas and language to find a name. Looking at the faces, local and foreign, lit by the firelight as they gesticulated their communications in broken French and Arabic, pigeon-English and Berber, I could see that the puppy had already enriched our lives.

The name we finally settled on was suggested because of our journey that day. We had come through a mountain pass called the "Tizi 'n 'Ourghsan," meaning Pass of the Teeth, and the word "*tizi*" came up regularly on our route, meaning a pass or saddle. All and sundry started chirping "Tizi" into the air and Tizi, obliviously pouncing from shoelace to shoelace, was christened.

In the warmth of the following morning Tizi had her first bath.

You could see the fleas leaping! She hated the experience of being wet. She stood dripping and shivering; her resentful glare one of the first indications of the strength of her character. I had to get back to a city to find any veterinary products for her, and most importantly a flea collar. After a wash, she turned out to be the palest gold color, fading to white at the muzzle. She was positively adorable, with big rich brown eyes. Everyone, including the Berbers, was enamored with her; she had emerged a happy, frisky, and inquisitive young dog, with enormous energy for play and an immediate recognition of our social group as her home.

I was surprised by how quickly she bonded with the trek group. She instantly understood the scenario of moving from camp to camp, the boundaries of the camp, and who was in our party and who was not. She had no previous experience of this, so I assumed it was a natural feature of her intelligence.

She was just a tiny puppy. Legs at three inches and weighing six pounds when she joined us, she had the enthusiasm for following along but was far too small to handle the 15 to 30 kilometers we walked each day. So, she was packed into the top of my rucksack, either when she was tiring, or for safety going through a village. The Berbers thought it hysterically funny that I would carry a dog on my back. The first day she managed just half a mile. Her eyes never left me, and her will to follow was obviously strong, but her weakness was evident; she was soon staggering and panting. With good food she gained strength quickly and grew fast. As she got heavier to carry, she could manage longer distances and became impatient with going in the rucksack. Most of the time it proved a reasonable balance: when she was tired she wouldn't mind the rucksack, when she wasn't, she could walk.

Sometimes we would have to do much longer distances or difficult mountain ascents. On these days it was too difficult for little Tizi to keep up with us and I couldn't carry her because of other equipment I had to carry or other safety aspects of my job. On these longer days I would hand her over to the muleteers and she would ride on the mules. She would arrive in camp strapped into washing bowls, or baskets, or held by a muleteer on his lap. She really detested the mule rides. I assumed it was the lack of freedom; she was generally tied into some restricted space so she couldn't jump off and hurt herself. As we went from trek to trek, she grew bigger and fitter, and by four months old she was lean and muscled and trekking the trails with ease, thankfully without mules.

One might suppose that a wild Moroccan village dog would eat anything. The dog population of Morocco teeters on the brink of starvation and survives by scavenging. As I got to know Tizi I could see how, although she was distinctly a mongrel, she had inherited certain strong traits which equipped her for this hostile environment. She needed almost no water, she managed on little food; she did scavenge, even though she was well fed—and she was mentally designed to cope with such a harsh life.

Psychologically, she was an enigma to me. I had spent many months with Huskies in Alaska, and had studied their psychology and wolf-pack sociology. I saw none of this in Tizi. The huskies had been open and devoted; loyal and keen to please. Tizi was distinctly different, and it seemed to me not just a matter of character but also of genetic provenance. This dog had a wildness of spirit and iron-hard will. She was born to scavenge amongst the rotting waste of the villages and to shy away from humans.

It was fascinating to ponder what wildness and independence was in her ancestry. Cleanliness, and being tied up, were anathema to Tizi. Her closeness to people was due to what she received from them in terms of food and shelter. She had little need for social interaction; growing older she played less and roamed more. Although I adored Tizi, she was not bonding with me. Her strongest feature was a ruthless independence and a stubborn willfulness to do her own thing.

As manager of the trek I was required to keep impeccable hygiene standards. This meant keeping Tizi clean and under control. Tizi's agenda was the opposite of mine, of course. She wanted to roam free. She couldn't be loose at night and would be kept on a leash at my tent. Sometimes she would curl up with me in my sleeping bag, which I loved; sometimes she would stay outside, and I would feel rejected. One thing was certain: she detested the leash and hated any restriction. Issues of hygiene centered around her mixing with other wild dogs, which she did at every opportunity, and then coming back into camp, possibly carrying parasites or diseases passed from them. She would refuse her food, purchased at great expense in Marrakech, and then be found covered in grime, dragging a sheep's head around at the edge of camp.

It was a big job to keep an eye on her, and as she got older she became wilder and more headstrong. Often I would see a sort of sullen obedience from her rather than happy compliance, as if her innate willfulness dictated some course of action that she knew impossible within the "rules," and the result was a limp dejection and resentful submission. I was troubled that perhaps this was not the best lifestyle for her, but she seemed so much to love the traveling and the people.

The local reaction to Tizi and me was intriguing. It was as if we had become film stars overnight. Village people would gasp and stare as I passed with this golden puppy poking out of my backpack. "*Aini*"—the Berber dialectal word for "dog"—was whispered behind me and, taken up by the children, became a chorus as they skipped alongside.

Soon, we became somewhat famous in the valleys of the High Atlas. I would hear "Tizi!" echo from the hillsides and the villagers would greet us, expectant and curious at this new feature from abroad. In Marrakech I was viewed as terribly eccentric. Suddenly Tizi was valuable; I was offered money for her from rich Moroccans. My trekking crew had overcome their prejudice, it seemed, and would play with Tizi and offer her treats.

It was not until late in the season that I began to suspect that things were not as they outwardly seemed with the Berbers (which I now know is a strong cultural characteristic), and I was to discover just how deeply my non-conformity was disapproved of and how little of that disapproval was shown to my face. I began to suspect that Tizi was not treated well when she was "looked after" by the Muslim staff. Tizi managed to tell me quite plainly herself one day. Sitting beside a well-used mule trail, with Tizi happily sniffing its edges, I noticed the string of our pack mules and muleteers approaching. Tizi stopped to watch them. As they arrived within ear-shot I hailed them, and as soon as Tizi realized who they were her whole body changed. Cowering she hung her head, crept behind my legs, pushing herself into me for my protection. I was deeply moved by her reaction, realizing this was no mere resistance to going on the mules, but a true fear of these men.

Later, I was told by a Berber friend that, although they were sweet to Tizi in front of me, the muleteers would beat and antagonize her while I was away. I was *furious*. But the frustrating truth was that I could only keep Tizi on trek with the Berbers' cooperation, so I made no mention of my knowledge but kept Tizi with me from then on.

As the end of my summer approached, I was desperate to find a new owner for Tizi. Many Moroccans offered to take her, but I could never trust them to care for her beyond my departure. There were no Europeans to turn to. I tried desperately to export Tizi to Britain, my home, or to Europe, but this proved impossible. I was wretched. I had spent almost every moment of this five-month summer with Tizi. I had watched her grow and knew her intimately. Her future was my responsibility and I could not guarantee her safety. And I loved my companion. I spent a week trying to make things work, throwing money at the problem and trying to keep Tizi as my own. But I had made commitments I couldn't be released from, in distant Asia where Tizi couldn't go.

It seemed to me that Tizi's fate had been determined the moment I met her. Her imminent torture and possible death, her helplessness and youth, the harsh culture and hostile environment, my wandering lifestyle and lack of means, all these factors combined to doom her from the start. Although I tried very, very hard, I was as helpless to change things as she was.

In the end I came to the arid conclusion that there was only one way I could be absolutely sure she didn't suffer when I left Morocco. I had given Tizi five very good months. She was healthy, fit, well-fed, happy, and had enjoyed a lifetime that she could not have expected from her beginnings. The only safe insurance that she would not suffer the torture, starvation, and maltreatment normal for her type was to have her painlessly put down by a vet before I left Morocco. I cried, agonized, had nightmares—but found no better solution.

I took Tizi to a charity clinic set up by the EEC in Marrakech for the protection of dogs. The vet there was volunteering his time and, I trusted, was dedicated to caring for dogs. He had given Tizi all her shots in puppyhood. In floods of tears I discussed my decision. He agreed but said that he would try to find her a good home first. I made him promise that he wouldn't give her up to become a guard dog in one of the thousand concrete yards attached to the homes of Marrakech. He persuaded me to leave Tizi with him, and I flew out of Morocco the next day.

I left Marrakech wretched at not knowing what did finally happen to Tizi. I dream of her often, haunted by that uncertainty. I try to soothe my conscience, knowing that I saved her from painful suffering, but I still agonize over whether I did the right thing. I'll never really know.

⋆

Wendy Smith, a native of the U.K., was once a personnel manager and army officer who is now a professional outdoor trainer and expedition leader. She has led treks on four continents. In 1998, Wendy completed an expedition by dog-team across Canada, making her the first person ever to mush coast to coast.

⁎ ⁎ ⁎

Remember Africa?

A life of travel bestows a final gift.

"WHO ARE YOU?" FRANK DEMANDED WHEN RUTH WALKED INTO the room. She sighed and eased gently down on the bed next to him, folding his age-shrunken hand in hers. He recoiled from her uncertainly, fear widening his eyes.

"I'm Ruth, your wife," she said, forcing a polite smile and patting his hand.

His eyebrows shot upward as he bolted upright in bed. "Wife?"

"We've been married forty years, Frank."

"No." Frank shook his head vigorously. "No. I don't remember you."

Ruth nodded and closed her eyes. It was a conversation they had had nearly every day during the past few months. The illness had not much weakened Frank's body, but his mind faded, day to day, like color from an oft-washed cloth.

"That's okay, dear," Ruth answered. "I love you whether you know me or not." She adjusted the pillow between his back and the wooden headboard, then straightened the covers around his waist. "Oh Frank, we've had so many wonderful years. We've sure had a good life together."

He smiled back at her tentatively, eyes still clouded in confusion.

"Was I a good husband?"

She chuckled. "You devil," she said, pinching his cheek softly. "The best. You were always kind and gentle and lots of fun. Even now, you try, don't you?"

He nodded. Her words seemed to reassure him. He looked around the room, as if desperately searching for clues. "Our family...?"

Ruth hesitated. "We never had children, Frank. We tried, but we couldn't. But we have so many friends and loved ones. You've lived eighty-two good, long years now. People have always loved you, Frank. And you've touched so many lives."

"Hmmm."

He nodded, but his eyes kept that faraway gaze, unable to connect with any familiar faces. "Well, what did we do?"

"Well, mister, we worked. We worked hard and we built up your family business and we went to church and we enjoyed ourselves just fine. And we traveled all over the world."

"Oh?" His eyes danced, just a flicker of light. "Where?"

"Everywhere, Frank. We went to so many beautiful places. Do you remember Edinburgh, Frank? The castles and the countryside of Scotland? You loved how green it was, even when we were freezing. And you wore this silly plaid cap that made me laugh." She searched his eyes, but the light had passed.

Frank slipped back down on the pillow and stared at the ceiling. His profile was nearly the same as her first sight of him 40 years earlier, as he stood in her doorway, coming to pick her up for a ride to church camp. When she opened that door, his eyes had grown wide with interest, and he gave her that devilish grin she'd come to love so much. Now his mouth was drawn tight, grim with irritation.

"And Japan. Remember Tokyo, Frank? Remember the lights and those crowded streets, and the temples? How you bought all those tiny mechanical toys, and the radio as small as your fingernail?"

She held up his hand to show him, but his eyes were squeezed tight, his mind fruitlessly searching for his memories. He shook his head, a frown deepening on his face.

A moment passed. He blinked and stared at her again, at the face he had awakened to every morning for 40 years.

His eyes narrowed. "Who are you?" he asked, his voice edged with fear.

She drew a long, steady breath, looking into his bewildered eyes. "Africa, Frank," she said slowly. She took his hand back, gripping it tightly. "Do you remember our travels through Africa?"

"Africa..." he repeated quietly.

"We saw animals..." she ventured softly.

"Lions..." he answered. She sat silently, waiting.

"We saw lions," he said, pulling himself up slowly beside her. "We sat in the Land Rover and the lions were surrounding us, coming right up to us. And there were elephants, and a huge one with the huge tusk that came crashing out of the bush right at us..."

Ruth nodded, smiling back at him.

"You were there with me. You were sitting next to me." His eyes were clearing, shining; she could feel the tears begin to well in her own.

"And the flamingoes," he said, his voice rising. "We stood at the edge of the lake and watched them fly. There were so many of them, it was just like a pink cloud rising up from the water."

His words slowed, and his eyes closed.

"Frank..." she said, and he sat still, not moving, not answering.

"Frank, remember the night in Uganda, when the children sang to us? We were in that little village near the river..."

"The children! Yes," he said, opening his eyes again. "They were so young, so sweet..."

"And their round little faces all lit up..."

"...they were all holding candles! And afterward, we ate in that man's home, with the dirt floor. We sat in the candle light, and they brought us the food in those huge black bowls..."

"Remember how strange that food looked?"

Frank laughed, then groaned. "We didn't know if it was raw, or worms, or what. And, and...were we with missionaries?"

She nodded. "Yes, we were visiting missionaries who had a church in the village."

"Yes, yes," he said. "I can see them now. And the missionary told us how he prayed before he ate. He prayed, 'Lord, I'll put it down if you keep it down!'"

As they laughed, she took in every detail—the blueness of his eyes, the curve of his cheekbones, the wrinkles surrounding his smile.

Then Frank looked toward the window, where sunlight streamed in through a crack in the curtains. "Ruth," he asked worriedly. "Why am I in bed so late this morning?"

"You're not well today, Frank."

"I am feeling tired," he said, yawning. He slid back down onto his pillow, smiling dreamily up at her. "Ruth, what were those waterfalls?"

"Victoria Falls?"

"Yes, Victoria Falls. Ruth, I remember standing there, feeling the spray from the falls, and you were scared and holding onto my arm so tight. And you said it was the most beautiful sight you had ever seen. And I told you no, you were still more beautiful to me."

He curled up and kissed her softly on the cheek. She was shaking, holding as tight to his arm as she had at the edge of the falls.

"And you still are beautiful."

"You are something else, mister," she laughed.

"I love you, Ruth."

"And I love you, Frank."

His eyes were blinking, fading.

"Why don't you dream about those waterfalls?" Ruth said. "I'll be right here."

With that, he gave a sigh and relaxed, his sparse gray hair flattening against the pillow.

Ruth pulled the covers up around his chest and kissed him, listening to his breath rise and fall. His mind was drifting back in the fog, away from her and the world they had shared. When he woke, he would again recoil from her. And she knew the sight of his face and the warmth of his skin were a gift, a brief glimpse too soon lost to memory. Someday, even the vast continent would not have the power to bring him back to her.

✷

Jo Beth McDaniel is a journalist and author living in Long Beach, California. Ruth and Frank are her great aunt and uncle. This essay is based on talks McDaniel had with her aunt Ruth. She says their story introduced her to the importance and mystery of travel.

PART FIVE

THE LAST WORD

ANDREW BILL

⋆ ⋆ ⋆

Just Desert

*The author learns one of
life's great lessons.*

AT THE TYPICAL MANHATTAN COCKTAIL PARTY, AS THE SUITS
mingle and admire, as kisses are exchanged and ambitious eyes flut-
ter around the room, the conversation curves around to the inevitable question: what do you do? I realize it's a positioning tactic,
a modern substitute for sniffing and howling. In this spirit, I answer
that I am a traveler. If pressed further, I tell them that since the age
of 17, from the first moment I had the finances, freedom, or both,
I have traveled. First around my native Britain, then across the
Channel on short "vacation" sorties into France. Then, like a child
that's interested only in its outer boundaries, I ventured further and
longer away from home. Until, at the age of 37, I have lived on
three continents and left my footprints in over 100 countries. As a
travel writer, I have made it my career, my passion, my character.
Traveling is what I am.

The next question—if there is one—is either "where's your
favorite place?" or "what was your worst moment?" The first I
just brush aside. The heart of the true traveler is fickle, promiscu-
ous. How can there be favorites when the whole motivation for
travel is shunning the familiar for the excitement of newness? In
response to the second question, I have many stories to tell.

Especially in the course of my early travels—when a lack of money and a lot of time necessitated hitchhiking through the night, sleeping in city parks or on lonely beaches—I have gathered a store of tales enough to fill a thousand cocktail parties. I have been cornered in the solid 2 a.m. shadows of the Greyhound Bus Station in Boston by a knife-wielding Irishman who, fired by the strong spirits of his homeland, was convinced "the only good Englishman was a dead Englishman." I have been shot at in the bright-red poppy fields of the Golden Triangle where Burma, Laos, and Thailand converge to form the opium capital of the world; framed and arrested in a small tropical "prawn" town in the north of Australia where just being a foreigner was tantamount to a confession of guilt. I have been given a death sentence by a doctor high in the Himalayas, and attacked by a wave of rats on a black night in Mexico. Yet among all these experiences there is one moment in the Sinai that stays lodged in the forefront of my memory like a bone in the throat. Remarkable not for its drama but for what it taught me about myself, it remains as fresh as the day it happened over 15 years ago.

"Masari?"

I shrug my shoulders to tell him I don't understand. Not that word. Not any word. I can't even look it up in my dictionary. It probably isn't Egyptian at all, but one of the many Bedouin dialects.

"Masari?" he says again, spitting out the word like an olive pit.

I look back at him, reading his face for clues. A dusty red-and-white checked headdress obscures all but the small oval from forehead to chin. Dirt has been ironed into a thousand lines by the desert and the sun. His eyes, even in the shadow of the room, are burnt into thin rheumy slits. Untamed jet-black eyebrows hint at the color of his hair. The lips are set in what can only be impatience, rapidly dissolving into anger. I can't tell what age he is, still less what he is saying.

"Masari?" he almost shouts it this time, *"Masari? Felous? Felous?"* It's obviously a question. Fumbling in the folds of his tunic, he extracts a disheveled Egyptian pound and waves it in my face.

Here it is. The moment I have been expecting for the last hour. Dreading. One thing I have learned from my few years on the road is that nothing is for nothing. It's exactly proportionate: the more foreign the country, the more I am regarded as a one-man walking business opportunity. The postcard that costs 5¢ to a local, costs $1 to me. The "set price" for the taxi ride from the airport magically inflates out of control as soon as I hit an open stretch of road. I'm perpetually on guard, seeing the rip-offs as obstacles to be avoided by the savvy traveler. The few times I get badly caught, I rationalize the loss. What does a dollar mean to me, after all, compared with its power in local currency. My simple camera is worth a year's worth of meals to a starving family. I have spent more on having a tooth capped than many Third World-ers will ever mass over a lifetime of grueling labor. And yet I feel a mounting indignation swelling inside, from a sense of my own gullibility, from allowing myself to be fooled like a common tourist.

But today I have committed the cardinal blunder. My caution overpowered by two days of aching hunger, I have accepted food and hospitality from a total stranger. Worse, he is a nomad, a desert dweller, dealing from a completely different deck of customs and values. For him "taking" is the same as "earning." And I followed him home, ate everything that was offered, and never agreed on a price in advance. Stupid! Stupid! Stupid! Now he is going to levy an enormous price—somewhere between my money and my life—on a few pieces of dehydrated bread, rubbery meat, and a tomato sucked dry by the sun. And the spirit in the sheep-bladder bottle would strip paint. Considering my choices, I look around the room.

We are sitting in what had been, just four months before, the living room of a modern, luxury condo. The place has been stripped to the bare walls leaving only a few hints of its former style. Chrome light fixtures in the shape of medieval torcheres hang upside down from wires as though someone had ripped them down in a hurry and given up half-way through. There is no electricity anyway. The broken-in door swings awkwardly on its hinges. The window panes are all broken and, caught by the late afternoon breeze off the sea, floral curtains wave out like flags. Dust covers everything in a softening film. In the middle of the green wall-to-wall shag carpet burns an open campfire made of broken drawers and paneling. Around its edge, the nylon weave is curling, sending up a black-smoke stench.

Around its edge lounge five other Bedouin men, all dressed in the same robes as my host, with traditional *okal* headdresses and the *khangars* at their belts. Clearly these half-swords are not just for show. Throughout the meal these men have looked over at me with dirty, gold-toothed smiles, obviously enjoying the game of ripping off the white-skinned foreigner. It occurs to me this is a familiar situation and I am probably not the first Westerner to be sharing this room and their food. If I run for the door, surely one of them will be there to block my exit. If not, I have no doubt, they will catch up with me in the streets below. The smiles will then be gone and who knows what will follow.

Seeing no alternative, I loosen the tails of my shirt, uncover and unzip my money belt. All my valuables are now on show. My watch, passport, the few traveler's checks I have, and the thick soiled wad of local currency. Glancing quickly at my host, I see his eyes widen. With my heart in my mouth I try to offset the inevitable. I say the one Egyptian word I know, *"bekam?"* (how much?).

The Sinai Peninsula is the huge triangle of desert dividing the two outstretched arms of the Red Sea. Above it teeters Israel; to the left, the great sprawl of Egypt. Its harsh, unforgiving lunar landscape is burnt as hard as a pot in a kiln. From a rugged mountainous interior, a boulder and scrub strewn terrain spills down to an unremarkable coast. One hue—beige. Until you dip one inch below the surface of the sea. As if all the color had drained into the water, there lies a marine world of unimaginable beauty.

In 1982 the Sinai was on the front page of every newspaper. After three years of "preparation," Israel had honored the terms of Begin and Sadat's Camp David Accords and handed back the region to Egypt. Along with the desert, Egypt inherited all the buildings and infrastructure that had sprung up over the previous decade when the coasts along the Gulfs of Aqaba and Suez had blossomed as the Riviera of the Middle East.

Naturally there was chaos. When the Israelis left they took everything with them. Everything that could be moved, unscrewed, dismantled or otherwise heaved on to flat-bed trucks and driven north. The pans and cookers from the hotel kitchens, the sinks and door knobs from the luxury apartments, the tiles from the walls, the contents of the luxury beach-front boutiques. And, of course they took all the food.

If I knew this at the time, I paid little attention. As a university student, my needs were simple and my tolerance for discomfort, high. Besides, my interest was far more Old Testament than media front page. For me the Sinai was the romantic bridge between Africa and Asia. It was birthplace of the alphabet, the stage-set of *Exodus*, where the seas had miraculously parted for the escaping Israelites, where God had spoken from the flames of a burning bush, where Moses had found and dropped the Ten Commandments, that summary of divine law. On another, more immediate level, the Sinai was also the site of the best scuba diving in the world. Compared with this, what could possibly be so bad?

Well, there was the temperature. In retrospect, August was probably not the best time to be carrying a 50-pound backpack through a desert described even by the guidebooks as "intensely hot." And there was the lack of any predictable transport. As I left the air-conditioned bars of Eilat, Israel, at my back and made my way on foot along the dusty road to the Egyptian border, the heat bore down on my head like a broiler, flooding the world with white heat, melting the horizon in a watery wash of quivering snakes.

At the border there were no crowds of flag-waving well-wishers, no congratulations, nothing of significance to mark my historic crossing but a few strands of barbed wire half-heartedly stretched across the road and curling off into the scrubby desert on either side. At the end of the hundred yards of no-man's land I came to the Egyptian line. To the left a soldier in a ragged uniform was sleeping off his lunch in the shade of the only tree. To the right, the border post—a banged-up shed like a Porta-Cabin.

Inside, another soldier barked a single word, *"felous,"* then remembering a few words of English, he repeated, "money, money." An official-looking sheet was thrust in my hands explaining in a collection of languages that everyone who passed across the border had to change an amount of dollars proportionate to the length of stay. No exceptions. Four days? Two hundred dollars—an incredible amount which to me translated into at least 20 days of travel under normal circumstances. I handed over all the currency I had—around 40 dollars—with a shrug. After a few minutes of furious tapping on a decrepit addition machine, the soldier handed back to me an inch thick wad of notes, so soiled I could hardly make out their denominations. Doubtless, there had been a small commission for the officer's time.

I soon found out that in the Sinai it didn't matter how much money you had because there was nowhere to spend it. When the bus finally arrived a few hours later, the fare to Nuwaybi cost the smallest note in my wad. For the next few hours I sat, crammed in with a sweating mass of humanity and sundry livestock, as the bus creaked and groaned through a flat, unchanging landscape. The image of a cold beer and a good meal swam through my half-waking mind like a mantra.

But when I finally arrived in Nuwaybi, the once glamorous resort on the Gulf of Aqaba, I found that it was shut. Closed. Not open. The neat grid of streets was lined with boarded up stores, weeds were growing rampant through the sidewalk. Eventually I managed to pick up some *falafel* (deep-fried chick pea balls) and some bread, as dehydrated as the desert itself. That night I slept on the beach, underneath the boardwalk, burrowing deep inside my oppressively-hot down sleeping bag to escape the clouds of mosquitoes.

As the days followed a similar course, I began to associate more and more with the plight of the Israelites. It may not have been 40 years of privation and hunger but, as I made my way south, it certainly felt like it. The towns of Dhahab and Nabq were empty shells, all the more melancholy for what they had been so recently. At least the Israelites had manna from heaven, whereas I was reduced to eating whatever I could find. A jar of jam for lunch, crackers for dinner, and one day—oh the luxury—some canned sardines. There wasn't even any diving to be had. The few dive shops that deserved the name were cobwebbed and dark, waiting for their equipment to arrive.

But it didn't matter because I had set my sights on the southernmost town of Sharm ash-Shaykh. Things would be different there, I was told. According to the guidebook, it was an oasis of civilization, studded with bars and restaurants. Furthermore it was the jumping-off point for the greatest dive site in the world. Under the surface at Ra's Muhammad, the very peak of the Sinai, the fish—hammerheads, black-tips, rays as big as bed quilts—were so plentiful, they blocked out the sun as the schools swam overhead.

Like any other mirage, the oasis of Sharm faded before my eyes, its promise evaporating into the dry sand as soon as I climbed from the bus one late afternoon. Like the towns that had gone before, an eerie vacancy haunted its main streets and beach-front, as if it was a film-set waiting for the extras to arrive. Gone were the tanned couples promenading, the tables spilling out of cafes onto the street, the bikini-ed beauties, the cool palm-decked lobbies of the big hotels. Gone were the expensive boats, the bars heaving with the apres-sun crowd. The only movement came from a few enduring old Mercedes kicking up clouds of dust and the occasional Bedouin leading camels on a tether. In the hollowed-out cavern of a store, I found a bearded German who told me, in broken English, he had come to start a scuba business but was now going back to Berlin to wait until the situation here improved. "Here there is no customers," he explained dejectedly. "If they come, they can stay nowhere, and eat nothing."

No food. I was so hungry by this stage, I was even ready to break my vow and choke down another *falafel* ball. So I started combing the back streets looking for a restaurant. The locals had to eat somewhere, didn't they? I approached a few people, but they only shook their heads or pointed off in a vague direction. It was then that I saw my Bedouin and asked him in polyglot—raising my hand to my mouth and shrugging my shoulders—if he knew of any food.

To my surprise he beckoned to me to follow. Staying thirty yards ahead of me with his long strides and flowing robes, he set off through a white maze of alleys. After each corner I became more disoriented, more and more concerned I was being led into some sort of trap. What was stopping this desert savage pulling me into a doorway and sliding his knife across my white throat? In my backpack there were surely items of clothing that would be of use or amusement. At each turn my guide turned and beckoned me on again as if anxious I would lose interest and turn around.

After fifteen minutes I was so lost, I had to keep going. Then suddenly he stopped and, without a smile, imitated my gesture of eating and pointed up some exterior stairs to an upstairs apartment in a block of luxury condos. I hesitated. He repeated the gesture and urged me on. On the second landing he pushed open a door that hung loose on its hinges; clearly it had been jimmied open. Walking into the room I smelt first the stench of singeing carpet, then, as my eyes grew accustomed to the smoke and darkness, I saw the group crouched around the fire. They looked up at us. Our friend explained and smiles broke out. Obviously they liked his plan.

For the next hour I sat aside from the main group, leaning against one of the walls. There was no attempt at conversation. Nobody spoke. In silence—as slowly and deliberately as if they always cooked their food on a fire in the middle of a carpet—the Bedouin pierced hunks of fresh meat on the end of their knives, roasted them over the embers, then slid them off onto clean slabs of paneling that one of them ripped off the wall. After adding fresh salad and bread, my host passed a mounded plate over to me. I was too hungry to wonder where the fresh food came from, what the meat was, or what my new friends were expecting in return. Only when the meal was over and the food had cleared my head, did I realize the bad situation I was in.

"Bekam?" I say again, fully expecting my host to dispense with formalities, reach in and empty my money belt.

After a long minute he repeats the word at the others as if it's the biggest joke he has heard in ages. He says it again, pointing at me. The Bedouin around the fire sit up to enjoy the scene. Gold-teeth glint in wide grins.

Nervously I take out one of the bigger bills and hold it out. But it's not enough. My host shakes his head. I take out more bills. Still he shakes his head. It happens a third time. Just when I'm about to hand over the entire wad, he leaps up and goes over to the air-conditioning unit below one of the windows. He struggles with it, twisting it from side to side, until it comes clear of the wall. Rummaging in the exposed insulation, he pulls out a simple black metal box and brings it over to me, placing it as gently as an egg in my hands. He signals me to open it, which I do, fearfully, bracing for a trick. It's full of money. I pick some up and look up inquiringly at the man's face. Seeing my confusion, he leans over and closes my fist around the pound notes I have drawn from the box. I look around at the others. They are smiling encouragement.

Suddenly I understand what's going on. The realization hits me like a slap. The blood rushes to my face as the great temple of my Westernized preconceptions and prejudices collapses in a heap around me. To them I am not a condescending rich kid on vacation or a gullible traveler ripe for exploitation. They simply see another nomad who is in need. They see a beggar. They are not trying to take my money. They are trying to give me theirs.

✳

To maintain his life-long travel habit, Andrew Bill has answered a variety of callings, including river guide, road sweeper, painter, waiter, farm hand, and construction laborer. As a journalist and editor he has scoured the globe for many of the world's most prominent magazines and guidebooks. He lives in New York with his family.

Acknowledgments

"*Mein Gott*, Miss Siripan" by Susan Fulop Kepner reprinted from *Travelers' Tales: Thailand*. Reprinted by permission of the author. Copyright © 1993 by Susan Fulop Kepner.

"The Khan Men of Agra" by Pamela Michael reprinted from *Travelers' Tales: A Woman's World*. Reprinted by permission of the author. Copyright © 1994 by Pamela Michael.

"No Distance in the Heart" by Thom Elkjer reprinted from *Travelers' Tales: The Road Within*. Reprinted by permission of the author. Copyright © 1997 by Thom Elkjer.

"Crossing the Linguistic Frontera" by Joel Simon reprinted from *Travelers' Tales: Mexico*. Reprinted by permission of the author. Copyright © 1994 by Joel Simon.

"Letting Life Happen" by David Yeadon reprinted from *Travelers' Tales: Spain*. Reprinted by permission of the author. Copyright © 1993 by David Yeadon.

"A Simple Touch" by Robert J. Matthews originally titled "A Simple Gift" reprinted from *Travelers' Tales: Nepal*. Reprinted by permission of the author. Copyright © 1997 by Robert J. Matthews.

"The Gift" by Joseph Diedrich reprinted from *Travelers' Tales: Paris*. Reprinted by permission of the author. Copyright © 1996 by Joseph Diedrich.

"Terry and the Monkey" by Terry Strother reprinted from *Travelers' Tales: A Woman's World*. Reprinted by permission of the author. Copyright © 1994 by Terry Strother.

"In a Soldier's Care" by Nancy Hill reprinted from *Travelers' Tales: Love & Romance*. Reprinted by permission of the author. Copyright © 1998 by Nancy Hill.

"Seeing Red" by Louis de Bernières reprinted from *Travelers' Tales: Spain*. Originally appearead in the August 1995 issue of *Harpers*. Reprinted by permission of the author. Copyright © 1995 by by Louis de Bernières.

"A Tibetan Picnic" by Barbara Banks reprinted from *Travelers' Tales: Food*. Reprinted by permission of the author. Copyright © 1996 by Barbara Banks.

"Paper Patterns" by Charles N. Barnard reprinted from T*ravelers' Tales: Hong Kong*. Reprinted by permission of author. Originally appeared in *Prime Time*. Copyright © 1993 by Charles N. Barnard.

"Road Scholars" by James O'Reilly reprinted from *Travelers' Tales: France*. Reprinted by permission of the author. Copyright © 1993 by James O'Reilly.

"Remember Africa?" by Jo Beth McDaniel reprinted from *Travelers' Tales: Love & Romance*. Reprinted by permission of the author. Copyright © 1998 by Jo Beth McDaniel.

"Just Desert" by Andrew Bill excerpted from *The Intentional Traveler,* a work-in-progress edited by Thomas C. Wilmer. Copyright © 1998 by Andrew Bill. Published by permission of the author.

About the Editors

Larry Habegger, executive editor of Travelers' Tales, has been writing about travel since 1980. He has visited almost fifty countries and six of the seven continents, traveling from the Arctic to equatorial rain forests, the Himalayas to the Dead Sea. In the early 1980s he co-authored mystery serials for the *San Francisco Examiner* with James O'Reilly, and since 1985 their syndicated column, "World Travel Watch," has appeared in newspapers in five countries and on WorldTravelWatch.com. As series editors of Travelers' Tales, they have worked on some eighty titles, winning many awards for excellence. Habegger regularly teaches the craft of travel writing at workshops and writers conferences, and he lives with his family on Telegraph Hill in San Francisco.

James O'Reilly, president and publisher of Travelers' Tales, was born in England and raised in San Francisco. He graduated from Dartmouth College in 1975 and wrote mystery serials before becoming a travel writer in the early 1980s. He's visited more than forty countries, along the way meditating with monks in Tibet, participating in West African voodoo rituals, living in the French Alps, and hanging out the laundry with nuns in Florence. He travels extensively with his wife, Wenda, and their three daughters. They live in Palo Alto, California, where they also publish art games and books for children at Birdcage Books (www.birdcagebooks.com).

Sean O'Reilly is director of special sales and editor-at-large for Travelers' Tales. He is a former seminarian, stockbroker, and prison instructor with a degree in Psychology. Author of the controversial book on men's behavior, *How to Manage Your DICK*, he is also the inventor of a safety device known as Johnny Upright. Widely traveled, Sean most recently completed a journey through China and Southeast Asia. He lives in Virginia with his wife and six children.

TRAVELERS' TALES

THE POWER OF A GOOD STORY

New Releases

THE BEST TRAVELERS' TALES 2004 — $16.95
True Stories from Around the World
Edited by James O'Reilly, Larry Habegger & Sean O'Reilly
The launch of a new annual collection presenting fresh, lively storytelling and compelling narrative to make the reader laugh, weep, and buy a plane ticket.

INDIA — $18.95
True Stories
Edited by James O'Reilly & Larry Habegger
"Travelers' Tales India is ravishing in the texture and variety of tales."
—*Foreign Service Journal*

A WOMAN'S EUROPE — $17.95
True Stories
Edited by Marybeth Bond
An exhilarating collection of inspirational, adventurous, and entertaining stories by women exploring the romantic continent of Europe. From the bestselling author Marybeth Bond.

WOMEN IN THE WILD — $17.95
True Stories of Adventure and Connection
Edited by Lucy McCauley
"A spiritual, moving, and totally female book to take you around the world and back." —*Mademoiselle*

CHINA — $18.95
True Stories
Edited by James O'Reilly, Larry Habegger & Sean O'Reilly
A must for any traveler to China, for anyone wanting to learn more about the Middle Kingdom, offering a breadth and depth of experience from both new and well-known authors; helps make the China experience unforgettable and transforming.

BRAZIL — $17.95
True Stories
Edited by Annette Haddad & Scott Doggett
Introduction by Alex Shoumatoff
"Only the lowest wattage dim bulb would visit Brazil without reading this book." —Tim Cahill, author of *Pass the Butterworms*

THE PENNY PINCHER'S PASSPORT TO LUXURY TRAVEL (2ND EDITION) — $14.95
The Art of Cultivating Preferred Customer Status
By Joel L. Widzer
Completely updated and revised, this 2nd edition of the popular guide to traveling like the rich and famous without being either describes, both philosophically and in practical terms, how to obtain luxurious travel benefits by building relationships with airlines and other travel companies.

Women's Travel

A WOMAN'S EUROPE $17.95
True Stories
Edited by Marybeth Bond
An exhilarating collection of inspirational, adventurous, and entertaining stories by women exploring the romantic continent of Europe. From the bestselling author Marybeth Bond.

WOMEN IN THE WILD $17.95
True Stories of Adventure and Connection
Edited by Lucy McCauley
"A spiritual, moving, and totally female book to take you around the world and back."
— *Mademoiselle*

A MOTHER'S WORLD $14.95
Journeys of the Heart
Edited by Marybeth Bond & Pamela Michael
"These stories remind us that motherhood is one of the great unifying forces in the world."
— *San Francisco Examiner*

A WOMAN'S WORLD $18.95
True Stories of Life on the Road
Edited by Marybeth Bond
Introduction by Dervla Murphy

— ★ ★ ★ —

Lowell Thomas Award
— *Best Travel Book*

A WOMAN'S PASSION FOR TRAVEL $17.95
More True Stories from A Woman's World
Edited by Marybeth Bond & Pamela Michael
"A diverse and gripping series of stories!"
— Arlene Blum, author of
Annapurna: A Woman's Place

Food

ADVENTURES IN WINE $17.95
True Stories of Vineyards and Vintages around the World
Edited by Thom Elkjer
Humanity, community, and brotherhood comprise the marvelous virtues of the wine world. This collection toasts the warmth and wonders of this large extended family in stories by travelers who are wine novices and experts alike.

HER FORK IN THE ROAD $16.95
Women Celebrate Food and Travel
Edited by Lisa Bach
A savory sampling of stories by the best writers in and out of the food and travel fields.

FOOD $18.95
A Taste of the Road
Edited by Richard Sterling
Introduction by Margo True

— ★ ★ ★ —

Silver Medal Winner of the Lowell Thomas Award
— *Best Travel Book*

THE ADVENTURE OF FOOD $17.95
True Stories of Eating Everything
Edited by Richard Sterling
"Bound to whet appetites for more than food." — *Publishers Weekly*

THE FEARLESS DINER $7.95
Travel Tips and Wisdom for Eating around the World
By Richard Sterling
Combines practical advice on foodstuffs, habits, and etiquette, with hilarious accounts of others' eating adventures.

Travel Humor

SAND IN MY BRA AND OTHER MISADVENTURES $14.95
Funny Women Write from the Road
Edited by Jennifer L. Leo
"A collection of ridiculous and sublime travel experiences."
—San Francisco Chronicle

LAST TROUT IN VENICE $14.95
The Far-Flung Escapades of an Accidental Adventurer
By Doug Lansky
"Traveling with Doug Lansky might result in a considerably shortened life expectancy...but what a way to go."
—Tony Wheeler, Lonely Planet Publications

HYENAS LAUGHED AT ME AND NOW I KNOW WHY $14.95
The Best of Travel Humor and Misadventure
Edited by Sean O'Reilly, Larry Habegger, and James O'Reilly
Hilarious, outrageous and reluctant voyagers indulge us with the best misadventures around the world.

NOT SO FUNNY WHEN IT HAPPENED $12.95
The Best of Travel Humor and Misadventure
Edited by Tim Cahill
Laugh with Bill Bryson, Dave Barry, Anne Lamott, Adair Lara, and many more.

THERE'S NO TOILET PAPER...ON THE ROAD LESS TRAVELED $12.95
The Best of Travel Humor and Misadventure
Edited by Doug Lansky

— ⋆ ⋆ ⋆ —

Humor Book of the Year
—Independent Publisher's Book Award

— ⋆ ⋆ ⋆ —

ForeWord Gold Medal Winner — Humor Book of the Year

Travelers' Tales Classics

COAST TO COAST $16.95
A Journey Across 1950s America
By Jan Morris
After reporting on the first Everest ascent in 1953, Morris spent a year journeying across the United States. In brilliant prose, Morris records with exuberance and curiosity a time of innocence in the U.S.

THE ROYAL ROAD TO ROMANCE $14.95
By Richard Halliburton
"Laughing at hardships, dreaming of beauty, ardent for adventure, Halliburton has managed to sing into the pages of this glorious book his own exultant spirit of youth and freedom."
— Chicago Post

TRADER HORN $16.95
A Young Man's Astounding Adventures in 19th Century Equatorial Africa
By Alfred Aloysius Horn
Here is the stuff of legends—thrills and danger, wild beasts, serpents, and savages. An unforgettable and vivid portrait of a vanished Africa.

UNBEATEN TRACKS IN JAPAN $14.95
By Isabella L. Bird
Isabella Bird was one of the most adventurous women travelers of the 19th century with journeys to Tibet, Canada, Korea, Turkey, Hawaii, and Japan. A fascinating read.

THE RIVERS RAN EAST $16.95
By Leonard Clark
Clark is the original Indiana Jones, telling the breathtaking story of his search for the legendary El Dorado gold in the Amazon.

Spiritual Travel

THE SPIRITUAL GIFTS OF TRAVEL $16.95
The Best of Travelers' Tales
Edited by James O'Reilly and Sean O'Reilly
Favorite stories of transformation on the road
that shows the myriad ways travel indelibly
alters our inner landscapes.

PILGRIMAGE $16.95
Adventures of the Spirit
Edited by Sean O'Reilly & James O'Reilly
Introduction by Phil Cousineau

ForeWord Silver Medal Winner
— Travel Book of the Year

THE ROAD WITHIN $18.95
**True Stories of Transformation
and the Soul**
*Edited by Sean O'Reilly, James O'Reilly &
Tim O'Reilly*

Independent Publisher's Book Award
—Best Travel Book

THE WAY OF THE WANDERER $14.95
Discover Your True Self Through Travel
By David Yeadon
Experience transformation through travel
with this delightful, illustrated collection by
award-winning author David Yeadon.

A WOMAN'S PATH $16.95
Women's Best Spiritual Travel Writing
*Edited by Lucy McCauley, Amy G. Carlson &
Jennifer Leo*
"A sensitive exploration of women's lives that
have been unexpectedly and spiritually
touched by travel experiences…. Highly
recommended."
—*Library Journal*

THE ULTIMATE JOURNEY $17.95
Inspiring Stories of Living and Dying
*James O'Reilly, Sean O'Reilly & Richard
Sterling*
"A glorious collection of writings about the
ultimate adventure. A book to keep by one's
bedside—and close to one's heart."
—Philip Zaleski, editor,
The Best Spiritual Writing series

Special Interest

THE BEST TRAVELERS' TALES 2004 $16.95
True Stories from Around the World
*Edited by James O'Reilly, Larry Habegger &
Sean O'Reilly*
The launch of a new annual collection pre-
senting fresh, lively storytelling and compelling
narrative to make the reader laugh, weep, and
buy a plane ticket.

TESTOSTERONE PLANET $17.95
True Stories from a Man's World
*Edited by Sean O'Reilly, Larry Habegger &
James O'Reilly*
Thrills and laughter with some of today's best
writers: Sebastian Junger, Tim Cahill, Bill
Bryson, and Jon Krakauer.

THE GIFT OF TRAVEL $14.95
The Best of Travelers' Tales
*Edited by Larry Habegger, James O'Reilly
& Sean O'Reilly*
"Like gourmet chefs in a French market, the
editors of Travelers' Tales pick, sift, and prod
their way through the weighty shelves of con-
temporary travel writing, creaming off the
very best."
—William Dalrymple, author of *City of Djinns*

DANGER! $17.95
True Stories of Trouble and Survival
*Edited by James O'Reilly, Larry Habegger &
Sean O'Reilly*
"Exciting…for those who enjoy living on the
edge or prefer to read the survival stories of
others, this is a good pick."
—*Library Journal*

365 TRAVEL $14.95
A Daily Book of Journeys, Meditations, and Adventures
Edited by Lisa Bach
An illuminating collection of travel wisdom and adventures that reminds us all of the lessons we learn while on the road.

THE GIFT OF RIVERS $14.95
True Stories of Life on the Water
Edited by Pamela Michael
Introduction by Robert Hass
...a soulful compendium of wonderful stories that illuminate, educate, inspire, and delight."
—David Brower, Chairman of Earth Island Institute

FAMILY TRAVEL $17.95
The Farther You Go, the Closer You Get
Edited by Laura Manske
"This is family travel at its finest."
—*Working Mother*

LOVE & ROMANCE $17.95
True Stories of Passion on the Road
Edited by Judith Babcock Wylie
"A wonderful book to read by a crackling fire."
—*Romantic Traveling*

THE GIFT OF BIRDS $17.95
True Encounters with Avian Spirits
Edited by Larry Habegger & Amy G. Carlson
"These are all wonderful, entertaining stories offering a *bird's-eye view!* of our avian friends."
—*Booklist*

A DOG'S WORLD $12.95
True Stories of Man's Best Friend on the Road
Edited by Christine Hunsicker
Introduction by Maria Goodavage

Travel Advice

THE PENNY PINCHER'S PASSPORT TO LUXURY TRAVEL $14.95
(2ND EDITION)
The Art of Cultivating Preferred Customer Status
By Joel L. Widzer
Completely updated and revised, this 2nd edition of the popular guide to traveling like the rich and famous without being either describes, both philosophically and in practical terms, how to obtain luxurious travel benefits by building relationships with airlines and other travel companies.

SAFETY AND SECURITY $12.95
FOR WOMEN WHO TRAVEL
By Sheila Swan & Peter Laufer
"An engaging book, with plenty of first-person stories about strategies women have used while traveling to feel safe but still find their way into a culture."
—*Chicago Herald*

THE FEARLESS SHOPPER $14.95
How to Get the Best Deals on the Planet
By Kathy Borrus
"Anyone who reads *The Fearless Shopper* will come away a smarter, more responsible shopper and a more curious, culturally attuned traveler."
—Jo Mancuso, *The Shopologist*

SHITTING PRETTY $12.95
How to Stay Clean and Healthy While Traveling
By Dr. Jane Wilson-Howarth
A light-hearted book about a serious subject for millions of travelers—staying healthy on the road—written by international health expert, Dr. Jane Wilson-Howarth.

GUTSY WOMEN $12.95
More Travel Tips and Wisdom for the Road
By Marybeth Bond
Second Edition
Packed with funny, instructive, and inspiring advice for women heading out to see the world.

GUTSY MAMAS $7.95
Travel Tips and Wisdom for Mothers on the Road
By Marybeth Bond
A delightful guide for mothers traveling with their children—or without them!

Destination Titles

ALASKA $18.95
Edited by Bill Sherwonit, Andromeda Romano-Lax, & Ellen Bielawski

AMERICA $19.95
Edited by Fred Setterberg

AMERICAN SOUTHWEST $17.95
Edited by Sean O'Reilly & James O'Reilly

AUSTRALIA $17.95
Edited by Larry Habegger

BRAZIL $17.95
Edited by Annette Haddad & Scott Doggett
Introduction by Alex Shoumatoff

CENTRAL AMERICA $17.95
Edited by Larry Habegger & Natanya Pearlman

CHINA $18.95
Edited by James O'Reilly, Larry Habegger & Sean O'Reilly

CUBA $17.95
Edited by Tom Miller

FRANCE $18.95
Edited by James O'Reilly, Larry Habegger & Sean O'Reilly

GRAND CANYON $17.95
Edited by Sean O'Reilly, James O'Reilly & Larry Habegger

GREECE $18.95
Edited by Larry Habegger, Sean O'Reilly & Brian Alexander

HAWAI'I $17.95
Edited by Rick & Marcie Carroll

HONG KONG $17.95
Edited by James O'Reilly, Larry Habegger & Sean O'Reilly

INDIA $18.95
Edited by James O'Reilly & Larry Habegger

IRELAND $18.95
Edited by James O'Reilly, Larry Habegger & Sean O'Reilly

ITALY $18.95
Edited by Anne Calcagno
Introduction by Jan Morris

JAPAN $17.95
Edited by Donald W. George & Amy G. Carlson

MEXICO $17.95
Edited by James O'Reilly & Larry Habegger

NEPAL $17.95
Edited by Rajendra S. Khadka

PARIS $18.95
Edited by James O'Reilly, Larry Habegger & Sean O'Reilly

PROVENCE $16.95
Edited by James O'Reilly & Tara Austen Weaver

SAN FRANCISCO $18.95
Edited by James O'Reilly, Larry Habegger & Sean O'Reilly

SPAIN $19.95
Edited by Lucy McCauley

THAILAND $18.95
Edited by James O'Reilly & Larry Habegger

TIBET $18.95
Edited by James O'Reilly & Larry Habegger

TURKEY $18.95
Edited by James Villers Jr.

TUSCANY $16.95
Edited by James O'Reilly & Tara Austen Weaver
Introduction by Anne Calcagno

Footsteps Series

THE FIRE NEVER DIES
**One Man's Raucous Romp Down the Road of Food,
Passion, and Adventure**
By Richard Sterling
"Sterling's writing is like spitfire, foursquare and jazzy with
crackle...." —*Kirkus Reviews*

$14.95

ONE YEAR OFF
**Leaving It All Behind for a Round-the-World Journey
with Our Children**
By David Elliot Cohen
A once-in-a-lifetime adventure generously shared, from the
author/editor of *America 24/7* and *A Day in the Life of Africa*

$14.95

THE WAY OF THE WANDERER
Discover Your True Self Through Travel
By David Yeadon
Experience transformation through travel with this delightful,
illustrated collection by award-winning author David Yeadon.

$14.95

TAKE ME WITH YOU
A Round-the-World Journey to Invite a Stranger Home
By Brad Newsham
"Newsham is an ideal guide. His journey, at heart, is into
humanity." —Pico Iyer, author of *The Global Soul*

$24.00

KITE STRINGS OF THE SOUTHERN CROSS
A Woman's Travel Odyssey
By Laurie Gough
Short-listed for the prestigious Thomas Cook Award, this is an
exquisite rendering of a young woman's search for meaning.

$14.95

ForeWord Silver Medal Winner
— *Travel Book of the Year*

—— ★ ★ ★ ——

THE SWORD OF HEAVEN
A Five Continent Odyssey to Save the World
By Mikkel Aaland
"Few books capture the soul of the road like The *Sword of
Heaven,* a sharp-edged, beautifully rendered memoir that will
inspire anyone."
—Phil Cousineau, author of *The Art of Pilgrimage*

$24.00

STORM
**A Motorcycle Journey of Love, Endurance,
and Transformation**
By Allen Noren
"Beautiful, tumultuous, deeply engaging and very satisfying.
Anyone who looks for truth in travel will find it here."
—Ted Simon, author of *Jupiter's Travels*

$24.00

ForeWord Gold Medal Winner
— *Travel Book of the Year*

—— ★ ★ ★ ——